My Father's Business

English Bradshaw

WriteMore Publications,
an imprint of Duncan & Duncan, Inc.

Copyright May 1996 © by English Bradshaw

WriteMore Publications
(an imprint of Duncan & Duncan, Inc., Publishers)
Mailing address: P.O. Box 1137, Edgewood, MD 21040
Telephone: 410-538-5580 Fax: 410-538-5584

Library of Congress Catalog Card Number: 95-61464

Bradshaw, English, 1940–
My Father's Business

1. Religious aspects 2. Christianity 3. Spiritual 4. Motivational/inspiration

ISBN: 1-887798-03-X

All rights reserved. No part of this book may be reproduced or transmitted in any form or by any means without the written permission of the publisher.

Characters in *My Father's Business* were invented by the author. Any resemblance to actual persons, living or dead, is purely coincidental.

9 8 7 6 5 4 3 2 1

Dedication

For My Sister, Lillie—
A Wonderful Person,
A Lovely Soul.

Chapters

	Preface	6
1	In The Beginning . . .	8
2	God Created . . .	20
3	The World . . .	28
4	And The Fall . . .	31
5	Let There Be Light . . .	43
6	And There Was Light . . .	50
7	The Least Of Them . . .	68
8	My Brethren . . .	77
9	Ye Shall Know . . .	81
10	The Truth . . .	89
11	From Dust Thou Came . . .	103

12	Be Fruitful . . .	112
13	To Dust Thou Shall Return . . .	125
14	A New Heaven . . .	146
15	And A New Earth . . .	159
16	About My Father's Business . . .	174
17	Upon This Rock . . .	187
18	I Will Build My Church . . .	205
19	Paradise . . .	218
	The Author	230

Preface

In passing over a mountain trail one's point of observation is often changed. Sometimes the traveler finds himself upon the edge of a precipice looking down into dark and narrow valleys. Sometimes he climbs the heights and looks abroad over a superb and varied panorama of grand peaks and broad horizons.

In our experiences of life, we find that everything related to our happiness depends upon our point of view. We may lift up our eyes unto the hills even when walking in the valley of the shadow. We have wings like the dove and we can fly away and be at rest. Or, we can dwell in the confines of personal suffering, or gain the high lands from which we can see the glory that excelleth all others in the universal life spread out before us.

The world is wearied with complaints of "hard times," "financial and personal depression," and "social discontent." We are always looking to the future for remedies that never come. Let us open our eyes to the possibilities of the present and lay aside the smoked glasses of prejudice and ignorance through which we have looked at life.

Prelude

Let us identify God and humanity as inseparably united. Let us learn to unfold our latent powers and study the higher gospel of a true world. Then we will perceive that the banquet of life is always prepared and unrestrictedly inviting.

We will see that nature herself goes out onto the highways and into the alleys to compel us to come in.

We will see that no one is really shut out from the feast except the self-exiled. We will see that the only cause of suffering is in the individual himself. And, we will also see that life is very true in love, opulence, and equity.

In putting the words to these pages, I have painfully transfused the real life of agony of a child who was lost in a whorl of familial abandonment and wonderment but persisted in searching for the holiest of the whole that was essential in the nurturing of his love and happiness.

The narrative is received through the eyes of a child after living his first 11 years under the brutality and tyranny in an orphanage. A tutorial relationship to develop his spiritual guidance and development is established between himself and a brother who was cast off as being "crazy" and whose legacy he imprinted in the child's mind to "preserve your right to think."

The child's social and emotional maturity which unlocked the doors to his pinnacle in life i.e., to search for truth and understanding, is provided by other members of this dysfunctional family.

I implore the readers to look intimately through my eyes and languish with me in the wisdom and understanding of my spirit's embrace. I ask you to place your hand in mine and come close most dear, as I draw you near, to a sacred place brazened with the tingly pricks of wisdom and understanding—the inner sanctums of your own precious thoughts.

English Bradshaw

One

In The Beginning . . .

"Acka backa doodle gimme cup 'o coffee, acka backa doodle."

"Charlie, git in dis house right dis minute and wash yo hans 'fo I skin the daylights outta yo lil ol yella behind. Mr. Peay will be here soon an' I needs to be ready."

"Yas mam."

I picked myself up out of the soil under the porch where I was playing in the fine sandy soil and singing the words to the game of "acka backa doodle," where my sister May and I were uprooting the sand lice from their little whirlpool homes by taking a straw and whirling it around into the little holes until they came out. We'd then put them into a jar and throw them on the big girls who fought us all the time.

Sometimes I would grab a handful of the lice with a fist full of sand and walk around with them. Or I'd put them in my pocket with the dirt so I would have some sort of protection from the other kids. We also made one of the kids named Echols eat one at one time.

"I'm coming Miss Pounds," as I unconsciously grabbed a

handful of sand and scampered across the porch, down the long hallway, past the sitting room, past the girls bathroom, and into Miss Pounds room to rub her down. She would always make me come to her room and rub her big, fat, jelly-roll thighs and arms. Miss Pounds was so big and ugly and nasty and stinking too. Moreover, somehow she liked me. I was her little pet and I got into many fights with the other children because she favored me.

On this day I forgot I had my fist full of dirt and as I crawled upon the bed to begin her rub down, I released the sand and the sand lice between her legs which startled her as she felt the little sand crabs crawling over her.

She yelped like a wounded water buffalo and looked "down there" between her smelly legs yelling, "Nigga, what you don' did to me!" She simultaneously back-handed me with a slap that sent me sprawling clear across the room. I ran and ducked for cover under the bed as she commenced to poke at me with a broomstick as she yelled, "Come out from under dat bed nigga, I'm gonna beat the s… outta ya. Mr. Peay will soon be heah and I ain't ready for 'em."

She threw the broom down and waddled across the hallway to wash herself off while mumbling, "I ain't through wit you yet nigga. I'm gonna whup yo lil ass into da middle 'o next week." As she left the room, I crawled out from under the bed and flew down the hall, past the girls bathroom, past the sitting room, out the front door and back under the front porch where I hid for the rest of the day.

Miss Pounds was the three-hundred pound matron for the Baby Cottage at the orphanage. Her job was to supervise the young children in the Baby Cottage. She only laid on her big fat behind and belted out orders to the forty little boys and girls who lived in the Cottage. She also managed to find some reason to "whup" somebody before we went to bed each night.

Beatings were a very common occurrence in the orphanage. If you did not get beaten by either Miss Pounds, Mr. Bullock, Mr. Garrett or Miss White, you certainly would not escape the lashes from the "Bald-Headed Champ," Mr. Peay, who was the superintendent of the orphanage, or even his wife Mrs. Peay.

I can never forget Poor Deedy. Deedy would get a "whupping" everyday because he was a bed wetter. Deedy wet his bed every night and wore out several mattresses. He was too scared to get up and go to the bath room at night and just laid there and pee'd all over himself. I hated him for this because Miss Pounds would wake all of us during the night and make us stand in line to pee.

She would stand over us to make sure that we did something. We'd be standing in line in the cold because the heat was turned off each night, waiting to pee. It never failed—somebody would always have to do a "number two" before it was my turn, and I would have to wait until he was finished.

Joe Lewis was usually the culprit, so we would rush to get ahead of him. I almost started to commit murder at a very early age once when I really had to "go" and Joe Lewis was sitting there grunting and groaning because he was constipated.

No matter how many times we were forced to get up during the night—sometimes two, sometimes three times to go pee, Deedy would still wet his bed.

I really looked forward to the day when I reached the age of ten years; then I would move to the Big Boys dorm where they didn't have to get up during the night.

Some of the other boys at the Baby cottage included, Lonnie (Scooter), Albert (Snipper—a little old yellow boy who always snitched on everybody), Henry (Cornrows—and if you **really** wanted to cuss him out, you said real fast; Massy-Peas-Cornrows-Spook!), Ferrel (Fish), Alvin (Booster—could steal your hat off your head and whom I used to fight all the time for messing with my sister), Modestine (Scrap), Jack (didn't have a nickname), Joe Lewis (Eeny Weeny), Bobbie (Preacher), Eldrine (Skunk), Robert (Shoe), and Echols (Rabbit).

The little girls also stayed in the Baby Cottage until they reached the age of ten years then they moved into the Big Girls dorm. Our sleeping quarters in the cottage were separated by a long hallway with Miss Pounds' room next to the girls quarters. The bathrooms were located on the hallways to each sleeping area, and you had to pass the bathrooms to get to the playroom and dining room and kitchen.

Leyla was my little heart-throb whom I used to steal biscuits and bobbie pins for. One day I was ordered to Miss Pounds' room and while on the way, I passed the girls bathroom where Leyla had just finished her little "business." I went past the partially opened door, and tiptoed back to peep at her as she was pulling up her little dirt smeared panties.

WOW!

I was sent into orbit and I knew that she saw me peeping because the next time she saw me she gave me this little sneaky smile while I stood there and throbbed all over.

It was a rugged life and some of the kids did not make it. Echols was beaten into unconsciousness by the superintendent and never recovered. Boys and girls were continually running away from there and were picked up by the police and brought back and were beaten mercilessly by the superintendent.

Sundays were especially bad for my sister and I because the parents of some of the children would come to visit them and bring them all sorts of good things including new shoes, pants, dresses, underwear, toothbrushes, and some money for candy. No one ever visited us and we'd go under the porch and peer out at the other families.

God is kind to children. He doesn't let them suffer long. We created a game of adoption. We made believe that some of the other families were our own. We'd adopt the parents of some of the other children that we liked, and pretended that they had come to visit us. We'd also share in the delight that these children had while they visited. We even enjoyed the same excitement they did when they wore their new clothes and other things their parents had given them. This game of deception eventually began to be amusing as well as almost real to us which made our situation more tolerable.

Christmas was always a time of great joy and great sorrow for us. On Christmas day, we all gathered in the chapel where the Christmas tree was installed and waited for our names to be called to receive the gifts that were stacked up in a huge mound surrounding it.

There were lots of gifts there including big boxes, long and slender boxes, bicycles, roller skates, footballs, baby dolls, stuffed animals, some coloring books, school supplies, new socks and shoes, new jackets and sweaters, new overalls and stocking caps, new dresses and underwear—just about everything.

As the names were called, the children raced up to receive

their gifts and returned to their seats with arm-loads of gifts. Some kids needed help to carry them all. My sister and I sat next to each other holding hands and hoping against hope that the next name called would be one of us. As the pile decreased, our hopes sank with it because our names were never called.

Nobody sent us anything. We had no gifts to receive except the universal stuffed red cheese cloth stocking which was given to all of us by the Salvation Army. The stocking contained one orange or an apple, a candy cane, a handkerchief, a toothbrush, tooth paste, a pencil, soap, a little box of raisins, and a little Bible. I gave my sister the apple. She gave me her Bible.

My sister May and I were almost inseparable. We formed a close alliance with each other for mutual protection from the older boys and girls who were constantly at war with each other.

We also used the sanctuary beneath the front porch as our place to escape from the beatings and fights that took place amongst the other kids. We'd go there and daydream about who our parents were and what we would like to be when we left the orphanage. It was our little paradise.

May would sometimes cry and I'd comfort her and tell her that no matter what would happen to us that we'd always be together, and that someday our parents would show up and take us home with them.

None of the other children knew about "our secret place" except Shoe. One day when May and I went there and we were greeted by a big sleek black snake. It sank its fangs deep into May's arm. May yelled and ran into me trying to escape causing me to bang my head against a support beam which created a "knot" on my forehead.

I ran to tell Miss Pounds that May had been bitten by a snake and when she saw the "knot" on my head, she beat me after accusing me of having been in a fight with someone. May was rushed to the hospital with a swollen arm and with great fear that she might lose her life.

Needless to say, we never returned to our little paradise. This event has never left my memory and the enmity I have with snakes.

The summers were crammed with fun for us. Our first treat was to go barefooted. My, does it feel good to the feet to run through the grass and sand with your toes clutching the earth after being bound all winter in worn-out smelly brogan shoes.

We'd go fishing for crawfish and tadpoles and minnows and catfish. When the blackberries were ripened, we formed a legion of little black soldiers and tackled the thorns so we could fill our bellies first, then the buckets we were issued.

We'd get our butts whipped for eating the berries every time we went. Our tongues were inspected by Miss Pounds and Mrs. Peay to see if they were stained from eating the berries. I got wise one day and decided to hide the crime by rubbing my tongue with a fistful of dirt. It didn't work and I got two beatings—one for eating the berries and one for eating the dirt.

Sometimes when we were out berry picking, we'd take off our clothes and sneak into the creek and swim. This all came to an instant conclusion when one day we were in the creek naked and a bull appeared and began to eat the berries we had left on the bank of the creek.

Deedy yelled, "A bull, a bull is eating the berries!"

In The Beginning...

We all began to yell and attempted to crawl out of the creek, but the bed of the creek consisted of smooth gray clay and was very slippery. One person would crawl up a bit and someone would pull him down trying to get out. We were just like a bunch of little black crabs in a basket trying to escape.

The water in the creek became murky white and we couldn't see the bottom of it and to compound our grief, a big black cotton-mouth water moccasin swam by.

Leyla fainted and Booster had to crawl on his hands and knees beneath the water to find her. She was rescued and we jumped out of the water and noticed that the our clothing was in the same spot as the bull.

Cornrows tried to sneak up behind the bull to grab some of our clothing. He succeeded in reaching a pile of clothing and started to run when the bull turned, pawed the ground and began to chase him. He had made one big mistake. As he ran he was carrying Booster's red shirt and it was waving in the wind.

He ran naked and yelling at the top of his voice through briar patches, thick underbrush, over into the pig pen, into the slop (startling the pigs as they were slumbering) and ducked under the barb wire fence just as the bull lowered his head for the charge.

The rest of us grabbed our clothing and ran into the woods where we dressed and returned to Miss Pounds with our buckets empty and yes, of course, we got our butts beat.

I didn't like to go berry picking because of one very great concern I had. Chiggers! These little red lice would get into your crotch, burrow themselves into your testes, and create the greatest discomfort imaginable. I would be scratching for days and no matter what I was doing and under what circumstances, I stopped immediately and scratched.

They seemed to become most agitated when I was in chapel listening to Mr. Peay preaching to us that the "Lord will bring you comfort" or when standing before the classroom reciting a homework assignment and all eyes were directed towards me. I scratched!

The treatment we received for this infestation was an application of a mixture of kerosene and undiluted disinfectant. Wow! When this solution met my testes, it felt as if I had been given a shot in the rear with a flame-thrower. It hurt!

I spent a lot of time with myself and my thoughts. I was called the "Worrier" by the teachers and supervisors. They said that it seemed to them that I always had "something on my mind."

I would go off to someplace alone and sometimes lie on the dry edges of Deedy's mattress and just drift away into daydreams while lying on my back looking up into the blue skies and making artistic images of the stark white clouds as they drifted overhead.

One day, when I was about eight years old, as I lay there, it appeared to me that two grey-bearded men dressed in Biblical clothing, appeared through the skies.

One man had a dark complexion and the other one was clearly a white man. I laid there as if in a trance and vividly saw the movements of their mouths as they seemed to be talking to me in words that were invisible and inaudible for me to understand. I was not afraid nor was I prone to share this experience with any other person, including my sister.

After that experience, I became even more contemplative than before. I became restive and began to read a lot. I began to notice and study everything around me. Good grades in school were automatic for me. I could remember the smallest details of conversations held several months or years previously.

My communication skills and perception became sharpened. All of my senses were used when I communicated with a person. I didn't have to look a person in the eyes in order to establish a "real connection."

The eyes told me nothing. I used my eyes to "hear" things and to listen to their minds. I used my ears to "see" things. Before a person approached me with a topic, I had an inkling as to what was going to be discussed. Or, during a conversation, I could anticipate the next words before they were spoken. And so, I became very impatient with "fluff" or plain old bull. I became preoccupied with knowing the truth. I could see a lie before I heard it. I even felt it at times.

In Sunday school we were taught the words: "Ye shall know the truth and the truth shall set you free." There were two words which caught my attention, "truth" and "free." I took those words to be very real. I detested a liar. A liar was a very dangerous person to me. If I knew that a person had lied to me, no matter how close we were as friends or how large or small the lie was, I'd drop them like a hot potato.

We were also told to be honest. I was more concerned with truth than honesty because I felt that honesty may or may not have anything to do with truth and it can be modified. I saw a lot of things happening around me and people were able to "get away with it because it was an 'honest' mistake." I felt that truth was more real to me and I stuck with it. Because of this, I suffered a great deal because sometimes it became a cutting sword and bared the ugliness of a situation and people didn't want to hear honesty or deal with it at times.

I was always busy doing more than one thing at a time and completing complex tasks within very short periods of time to the amazement of other people. I began to question not only myself and others whom I thought had answers to where I came from. No one knew. I was told I had no parents, yet the other children had parents. Baby squirrels had parents. Where were mine? The children always teased my sister and me saying we didn't have any parents. Well if we didn't have parents, then how did we get here?

When I grew to the age of ten and discovered that I had other parents outside of the orphanage, I began to run away in search of them. I was returned and beaten but I kept at it. I decided that I would not stay there and I would not take any more beatings from Mr. Peay.

Our last encounter took place in the basement of his home when I was summoned to strip down to my underwear without a shirt. Mr. Peay also stripped to his waist and lunged at me with the horse strap he used on us. I grabbed the strap and with every ounce of strength I could muster, I yanked it from him which threw him off balance and he fell to the floor. Instinctively, I reached for a garden rake that was in the corner and swung it to his face.

The teeth of the rake sank into his face and neck and a fountain of blood gushed out that scared the living daylights out of both of us. He yelled to his wife for help who immediately rushed him to the hospital and his wretched life was spared by less that two minutes because of loss of blood.

I was told by Mrs. Peay not to mention what happened and Mr. Peay would not bother me again and they would do all they could to locate my parents. One year later, May and I were headed north to a big city in Massachusetts where we met our parents and other brothers and sisters.

While in the orphanage, we attended chapel every Sunday and vesper services on Wednesday nights. Mr. Peay conducted the services and I saw a great contradiction between his meanness and inhumanity towards us during the weekdays and his preaching the love of God to us on Sundays. I loved to go anyhow because it gave me the opportunity to read new stories and learn new words.

The Adam and Eve story fascinated me tremendously. I read it over and over again. Several versions of the same story were conjured in my mind each time I read it.

Two

God Created . . .

Upon reading the Creation and learning that Adam and Eve were the first parents to all of us, I felt a bit better. I also felt better when I learned that Jesus was born in a barn and grew up to be famous and that he died on the cross for the forgiveness of my sins because I was constantly being told that I would burn in hell when I died for being such a devil.

As I recall my favorite version, in the section called **The Creation of Man**, the Bible states that:

In the beginning God created the heaven and the earth. And the earth was without form, and void. All was darkness, confusion and watery chaos. And God said: "Let there be light. And there was light. And God saw the light, that it was good. And He divided the wondrous light called Day from the darkness called Night.

He also parted the waters of the firmament called heaven from the waters beneath upon the earth. (Now this puzzled me. I have never found the true meaning of the word "firmament." It is said by *Webster* to mean "vault of heaven; sky or support".) After the parting of the waters, dry land appeared with its desolate plains, arid deserts, thunderous volcanoes, and ice-capped mountains.

And God made the green seedlings to grow into grass, and herbs and trees yielding fruit; and He saw it and it was good.

In the heavens above, He set the sun and moon to shine and to lighten up the whole world. The sun ruled the day. The moon ruled the night, and the wandering planets each had its circuit into heaven. And God said let there be light. And there was light. He saw it and it was good.

Then God said:

Let the waters bring forth abundantly moving creatures that have life, and winged birds that can fly. So there were fishes in the deep sea—whales, sharks, and tuna. And in the crystal waters of the rivers and streams swam fish curious and marvelous in scale and fin and were swift in motion—salmon and sardines. And the air was sweet with birds—eagles, crows, buzzards, and sparrows.

And when God had given life to all his creation; tree and plant and flower and herb—from the towering cedar to the tumbleweed; all the creeping things and the insects, each where it would be easy to get its natural food for its strength—from the beasts so mighty and ponderous to the grasshopper shrilling in the sunshine on his blade of grass; and the silent lovely butterfly sipping her nectar in the flowers—and had finished his work in seven days and saw that it was good, he blessed it and bade all living things to grow and increase and be fruitful and multiply, then he rested.

Whew!

But something was missing. In all his wisdom, He was not satisfied with the earth until last of all living things, He made man and called him Adam.

Adam, shaped from dust and spittle, and given divine breath was different from every other living thing upon the earth. He was miraculous in grace and life and strength. His deep dark lighted eyes, his hair, his hands, the mystery of his beating heart, his senses to touch and taste and smell and hear and see—the miraculous wonder of his mind, made him different from the rest of the living creatures. And to top it all, he was made in the image and likeness of the Divine. This made Adam just a little lower than the angels of heaven, who were not from the earth but from a different being and nature, and who also dwelled in glory beyond thought or imagination.

Since Adam's body, like the other beasts was also of the earth, he was at peace with all of the creatures. God made him lord and master and to have dominion over all of them. And God said to Adam:

Lo, all these things I have made for your company and I will give you their charge to keep and to tend and to use. Do with them as your heart desires.

Through his eyes shone the light of day. He was clothed in the light and heat of the sun, and stood erect and moved his limbs and stretched his arms over his head and picked his nose.

His voice blended in harmonious **"wah la woo wah"** melodies as he sang in solo falsetto with the owls and the nightingale. He heard the voice of the beasts and the birds and fish and could communicate with them. And God looked upon him with love and said it was good.

For a dwelling place, God planted a garden for him. It was a paradise of all delight. This garden lay eastward in a place called Eden and a river flowed out from it to form the four great rivers of the world.

The name of the first river was Pison, now the Nile, which encompassed the whole land of Egypt where there is gold, a spicy bitter-sweet gum called bdellium, and the clear green onyx and beryl stone. The second river was called Gihon which encompassed Ethiopia. The third river was the Tigris, and the fourth great river was the Euphrates.

Since millions of years have changed the landscape, it is now impossible to return to the paradise of Eden via any of these rivers, except some would argue, the Euphrates.

In the midst of the Garden were two trees, secret and wondrous; the Tree of Life, and the Tree of the Knowledge of Good and Evil. Their branches rose in a silence so profound that not even the sound of birds or beasts could be heard there. And God again reminded Adam that He had given him all of the herbs he could ever want for food whose seed was in itself and of its own kind so that very tree could yield fruit and seed. And they did so abundantly.

He told Adam that he could freely eat of the fruit of every tree except the fruit from the Tree of Knowledge of Good and Evil and the Tree of Life. He was also told that if he ate the fruit it would bring him only grief and misery, and the day that he ate the fruit he would surely die.

Adam listened to these words with all his understanding and education. In his estimation it was the will of the Lord that he be free and peaceful. And so he obeyed the Lord.

The days of his life went by and Adam was provided with every thing his heart desired. For his company he had every beast of the field and every fowl of the air. To every living thing he gave a name, and whatsoever according to his exclamations of wonder, surprise, or delight, Adam called them by name—like the wombat, the yak, and the wallaby.

Its name and its image were memorized in his mind. At the call of each creature, it came fearlessly to his side. And he rejoiced. He called the mosquito and it buzzed by, the aardvark and it scooped up a snout full of ants, the kiwi who couldn't decide whether to fly or walk, the orangutan who pounded his chest into fearful masculinity, and the baboon who burst into laughter upon hearing such a name. They all cuddled up next to him in glee.

And Adam looked upon them, marvelling as they moved before him, each with his own kind following the desires of their heart and the instinct of nature and the secret of life when two creatures meet.

As Adam looked upon them, it seemed that he also shared in the life and being of each one of them through his insight and divination. They wandered amid the branches of the trees, browsing in the herbage, and on the gentle slopes at the river's brink they stooped their heads to quench their thirst, or stretched themselves to drowse in the sunshine, or lay cleaning and preening their sleek coats, or sported in play with one another.

Adam watched the birds among the green-leafed branches and glanced at the bees shuffling to and fro amongst the blooming flowers. For some reason, uncertain to himself, he was especially attracted to the birds and the bees. The swan with snow-white plumage, and the geese winging in the company of their kind were also observed. In the warm silence and the hush of night, the little owl called to him **whoo-a-whoo**. The nightingale sang whether the moon shone or not. Adam listened to them, never wearying of their cries and songs. He rejoiced, and the sound of his laughter in the Garden itself seemed to rejoice and to renew its life.

In the cool of the evening, God would return to the Garden and talk with Adam. And even when Adam slept, his divine presence was with him, and when he awoke to day, again his love enfolded him. Adam, in appreciation, praised God in everything that he did.

But the joy he found in the company of the creatures around him in the Garden, Adam had none like himself with whom he could share his own spirit and nature as a man. He was apart from the animals and was alone.

Eventually God read his mind as he was watching the beasts do their mating dance, and compassionately said:

No, this is not good that the man whom I have created should be alone. I had better hurry and make him a help mate. It is too early in history for any monkey business, except among the monkeys.

And in the darkness of night God caused a deep

sleep to fall upon Adam, and out of his side as he slept he took a rib from him and with a touch, closed and healed the wounded side.

Just as He had made all things living and Adam himself out of the dust, He, in the mystery of His wisdom, made woman out of man. He breathed into her body the breathe of life, and in the stillness of night she lay beside Adam as he slept. And the Lord looked upon her, and saw it was good to behold.

When daylight broke again over Eden and the shafts of sunrise pierced the eastern skies, the crowing of the rooster stole sweetly and wildly upon Adam's dreams. He awoke and saw the woman. She lay quiet as a stone, naked, the gold of the sun mingled with the gold of her body, her countenance was calm and marvelous.

Adam blinked his eyes, rubbed them, slapped himself in the face, scratched his head, dusted his hair, and stooped in awe and wonder over her. With his finger he touched her hand, and she arose.

She looked upon Adam and he at her, and out of one paradise he gazed into another. Love breathed in him, seeing that she was of his own form and likeness. And they went into a smiling period as he looked upon her. He shuffled his feet, and cried with joy, "Ooh La...Wah La Woo Wah, this is bone of my bones and flesh of my flesh. Thank you God!"

The birds chirped louder, and the bees buzzed heavier. So Adam was no longer alone in the Garden. He called her woman because she had been created by the Lord out of man to be his continual company and delight. She was Eve—Adam's wife. The world's First

Family. The two were one.

While in the paradise of Eden they romped and played in their nakedness, for they were as innocent as little children, and they were not ashamed. Happy and at peace with each other beyond the comprehension of any man's heart, they dwelt in the Garden, tending and dressing it to keep it fair and wonderful. The end.

How marvelous!

Three

The World . . .

The words to this story completely enraptured me every time I read it, or heard Miss White tell it to us in Sunday school. As I listened to the story, I looked around me and began to point out some of the similarities in my life.

There were fruits and vegetables and animals grown on the farm at the orphanage which was located adjacent to the main campus and supplied us with every food need we wanted—apples, peaches, strawberries, blackberries, green beans, snap beans, okra, black-eyed peas, onions, watermelons, squash, hickory nuts, walnuts, sweet potatoes, white potatoes, tomatoes, milk, chickens, eggs, chitlins, and pork chops.

However, there were in particular, two apple trees which grew on the main campus right next to the main administration building where the chapel was located and where Mr. Peay lived which gave him plain view of the area surrounding these trees. We were strictly forbidden to eat any of the apples from these two trees, even if they fell on the ground. We could not even go near the trees without getting the worst beating you could think of.

Mr. Peay especially and personally meted out this punishment because he felt that we were stealing from him and were disobeying his orders. But most importantly, these apples belonged to Mr. and Mrs. Peay and the rest of the supervisors. We were guided by three sets of rules which were strictly enforced—not to steal; not to lie; and not to disobey grown-ups.

One of the trees which was situated next to the chapel was enclosed in a plot of land surrounded by thick hedges and planted with roses and beautiful flowers and attended to by Mrs. Peay as her own personal garden. We were not to be caught in this area, even though it provided a shortcut from one part of the campus to the other.

Nothing which man has ever made was "Booster-proof." Booster would daily sneak beneath the bushes and steal the apples, and just as sure as day, he'd get caught and get his behind whupped. Those whuppings still did not deter him from continually stealing the apples.

One day Booster was up in the tree when Mrs. Peay came into the garden and he was trapped. He sat there quiet as a house mouse holding on and blending into the tree for nearly two hours. He didn't move a muscle for two hours. I doubt if he even breathed. The only thing which prevented him from continuing to steal the apples was an incident which occurred one Sunday afternoon when we were playing baseball against some white boys who evidently liked to get beat in every game they played against us.

Everyone's attention was directed towards the game when we suddenly heard a yell and the sound of breaking branches coming from the direction of Mrs. Peay's apple tree. Instantly, Booster crashed through the thicket of hedges with scratches on his face and arms and with torn britches and shirt, yelling,

"Snake, snake!" Sure enough, we captured a big green snake from the bushes, and from that day forward, neither Booster nor myself or any of the other children would go near the area. Cornrows said Mr. Peay put the snake in the tree to keep Booster out of it.

My favorite place to sit in the chapel was next to the window on the long wooden benches so I could gaze out at the beautiful, red, succulent, luscious, tempting, seductive, juicy apples as they waved defiantly at me while we sang "Swing Low" and prayed, "Give us this day our daily bread." This seat also gave me a clear view of one of God's greatest creations; my Eve and beautiful heart-throb—Leyla.

Four

And The Fall . . .

A s I think of the snake, Leyla, and the apples, I also recalled the rest of the story which was just as fascinating. This portion was called **The Fall From Grace**. It began:

Now of all the living creatures in Eden, the serpent was the most subtle. And because of his subtlety, he had in him the knowledge and malice of an angel who had fallen from God's grace because of pride. Adam did not know this. Neither did Eve. The serpent would drowse beside them and play with them.

Since the time when Eve appeared on the scene, Adam began to play with the snake more often as Eve watched. He would stroke its head and the snake would couch in his beauty upon his coils, cold and stealthy and with the changing color of his scales rippling his whole body, he would lift his head and seek their company.

He listened to them talk and watched them as they laid in their naked embrace playing and kissing and enjoying each other in the course of carrying out their natural tendencies as man and woman.

Envy sprang up in him. He hated them for their innocence and their peace and their happy obedience to God who gave them complete freedom to do as they wished. He would go off into the night and beat himself against a tree until he was satisfied.

One day, there came an hour in the fullness of morning when Adam was away from Eve. The serpent saw him leave and he approached her as she sat in the dappled shade from the sun after bathing in the cold waters to cool her body from the heat. She was rubbing her nude body with the soothing oil of the jasmine and had seen her own image in the reflection of the glassy waters and praised God for making her so beautiful.

The serpent, watching all of this became excited and envious. He flicked his tongue, lifted his head and fixed his eyes upon her as she sat brushing her hair.

He said in his low, husky, and most masculine voice: "Where's your husband?"

"He's gone into the glade to gather fruit from the Garden for us to eat."

"Good."

The serpent couched lower, peered through the underbrush, and rippled the scales upon his skin and cunningly said to her:

"Didn't God forbid you and Adam to eat the fruit of any of the trees in the Garden?"

Eve smile, amazed that the serpent could speak and said:

"No, we may eat the fruit of any tree in the Garden except from the Tree that is in the middle of it. God told us that we should not taste it or we would surely die."

And The Fall...

The Garden was still. Above them the wondrous blue of morning was brimmed with the light of day, and the shadows of the trees and mountains moved with the sun.

Except for the warbling of birds, and the humming of bees in the flowers, there was no sound between them. The serpent then crawled upon her and sat in her lap, drew back his head and looked at her—the loveliest of all things on earth that God had made, and from his cold and changeless eyes thrust a look into her that transfixed her into another state of nature which she had heretofore never experienced. The look which he gave her made her feel as if her entire body would explode.

He, being the most subtle of all creatures, knew that he had gotten her interested, then answered:

Yes, I know the Lord has said what He said, but be sure, that you will not surely die. For He knows full well that in the day that you eat the fruit of this Tree, then your eyes shall be opened to His wisdom and you will be as divine as Him and His angels, knowing both good and evil. Haven't you wondered why He forbade you from eating the fruit?

Think about it for just a second. Right now you have not even tasted or smelled its fragrance, but you just demonstrated to me that you share the same knowledge that I do. All I want to do is to show you how sweet and delectable the fruits are that grow upon this strange Tree's branches.

Eve listened to his guile. She did feel a little strange though. She stooped her head upon her shoulders and thought deeply within herself about what the serpent had said. And most importantly, she still remembered that look. The serpent, watching her remained silent. She finally said to him:

Oh, I don't know. I don't know what to do. I do feel a bit torn inside. My husband Adam, has expressly told me not to even try to find it, or even to look upon it. I don't even know where it is located. It is well enough for me that the Lord has told us not to eat from it unless we want evil to come upon us.

"Yes," said the serpent:

Your husband Adam knows where it is and has seen it. I know where it grows, come now let me show you where this Tree of Knowledge grows. Let us go together and you can see for yourself how harmless it is. Yes, it is true that it far surpasses every other tree in the Garden and when I myself quaffed in its fragrance, there was no one who could say no to me. But it may be that you have no thirst for this wisdom and knowledge, and your husband Adam may just be wanting to keep it from you and he can keep it all for himself. Come now, just to know where the Tree is located and to gaze upon it would certainly do you no harm.

Eve rose to her feet with trembling hands and looked around to see if she could find Adam. He was not to be found. The serpent had gone from her presence and was on his way when she yelled in a faint cry after him to wait for her. They both went with the serpent leading the way.

The way was very strange to her and it became stranger as they traveled. It narrowed between lofty trees whose upper branches interlaced to lock out the noonday sun. The ground rose steeply with lots of crags and boulders. They descended into a ravine where streams of water brawled among the rocks, separated, then met again into streams of calm pools. Birds of paradise showing their smoldering and fiery plumage so small that they seemed to be made of flames, and butterflies with damask wings hovered over the wide-brimmed flowers.

Soon the terrain changed and there were no more birds or anything living, and so in silence they continued on their upward climb where they had now reached the secret places of the Garden. In the hidden shade so deep, the air was cold and there was not even the sighing of the wind to cool her cheeks. It was so silent that she seemed to have heard the music of voices far off into the distance as if it came out from the mist of the firmament. She paused to listen. The serpent sat beside her while she rested. She entreated him with her eyes because her mind was troubled, but she would not speak to him. Speech was over between them. She just followed him again.

They came out from the shade of the forest into a hollow space of a marvelous verdure that fell away. It then rose in slope towards a mountain that towered high beyond it in the far distance. Beyond it, there was a light that seemed too rare and radiant for ordinary daylight and transfigured it into a vista of celestial wonderment. On either side of the mountain were rocks illumined with the colors of bright stone with a multitude of flowers mantled over them. Eve gazed into the vacancy of space. It was as though they had come to the earth's end.

Midway on the green of the mountain slope was a Tree—the Tree of the Knowledge of Good and Evil, while up above it, almost invisible in the light that shone upon it, was another Tree.

The faint sounds of voices and instruments of music from the distance had stopped. It seemed as though the radiant blue had been lost to the effluent vision of the light of heaven.

The serpent whispered into Eve's ear. "I thought I heard the sound of voices, but all is still and there is nobody here to watch us or hear us, so let us move on."

Eve approached the Tree whose branches were as of crystal and were ravishing to her eyes. Buds and petalled flowers lay open upon them, and they were burdened with fruit, both ripening and ripe. A nectar-like fragrance lay upon the air and Eve quaffed it into her nostrils.

The Tree was so beautiful that it created a strangeness in her body and made her heart pine within her, for the fruit was beautiful, pleasant, and desirable to the sight. Eve looked upon it and thirsted, even though a voice of her mind called a warning to her of the deathly and infinite danger she was in. Somehow the words of God and Adam were at a distance, although she knew them, she did not heed them.

The eyes of the serpent were fixed upon her and she succumbed to a feeling of reckless abandonment which came upon her senses. She put out her hand and fondled one of the fruits that hung low from the Tree and raised it to her lips. Its odor filled her with its desire. She plucked it, tasted it, and ate it, shuddering at each bite of its potency that coursed through her body.

She became without motion, then suddenly, the muscles to her abdomen contracted into thunderous vibrations. Her hips locked into a vice of frozen metal. She emitted a few shouts of mournful agony, exhaled an atmosphere of spent desire, then fell to the ground as if in a deep sleep. All life seemed to have ebbed from her body.

She awoke, and with her long gentle hand, methodically straightened her appearance and like the serpent, supple and undaunted, languished in her own beauty. She raised her head and stared with her eyes, exulting and defiant.

The radiance of the mountain which once dazzled her with its brilliance, now smote her with darkness. Dread and astonishment came upon her, and in fear, she turned to the serpent for help. She was repelled by the serpent, for the first time she felt alone.

She called for Adam, but he was not there. She didn't have direct communication with God—only through the man—Adam. So she grabbed the fruit that she had plucked from the forbidden branches and fled.

The darkness of the forest became cold to her body as she fled back by the route she had come. Stumbling and falling and rising again, searching for a way which she did not know, she continued to flee. She had no idea of why she was fleeing, but only to escape from the wild tumult of her mind. Her naked limbs were bruised, and her breath was spent as she came into the presence of her husband Adam who had been looking for her.

She had a strange and bleak look on her face as she crouched kneeling before him and thrust the fruit into his hand, and said, "See, see, the wonder that the serpent has been telling us about, has been given to me! Here, taste and see."

The sound of her voice was strange to him. He trembled at the sight of her face and became utterly loathful because he loved her. Without speaking a word, he took the fruit from her and paid no attention to the voice within him and ate it.

In that moment they knew that they had sinned. Their eyes were opened. They looked out at the Garden and all things that were once familiar to them were now estranged and remote. They had a new set of emotions which they had never experienced before.

Power was in their minds but it was not for the power of love but for the power of knowledge. They began to experience a new grief. They looked upon each other in fear and in horror.

Shame overshadowed them as they saw they were naked, yet they did not know where to turn to hide from their nakedness and shame. They plucked off leaves from a fig tree and sewed them together to make clothes to cover their bodies.

Smitten with doubt and confusion, they turned away from each other, and the love that was once between them had faded away from their faces like the dew that vanishes in the heat of the day. Burning, shaken with fear, yet on fire with life, they sat with their minds in torment. They dared not to raise their horror-stricken eyes to each other. They turned again as if they were seeking refuge for each other. Eve hid her face in Adam's hands and they wept.

Night drew near. The rays of the sun streaked with

the shadow in the valley where they sat. The milk-white flowers at their feet were now dyed with red. The firmament above them was flooded with a continuum of flames of orange. The song of the birds rose to a babbling rhapsody. The serpent appeared from a distance and yelled: "Hail, wise and happy fellowmen!" then disappeared. They looked at him with scorn in their eyes as they heard God walking in the Garden in the cool of the day. They were so afraid and hid themselves from his presence amongst the trees. And God called out to Adam, "Adam, where art though?"

The sound of His voice which at one time was their life and joy, instilled terror in their hearts. They came out from where they were hiding and Adam bowed his head because he could not look God in the face, and said, "I heard Thy voice in the Garden and I was afraid because I was naked and I hid my self."

God said to Adam, "Who told you that you were naked? Have you eaten of the fruit of the Tree, whereof I commanded you that you should not eat?"

Adam bowed his head a little lower and said, "The woman whom You gave to be with me, she gave me the fruit of the Tree, and yes I did eat."

And God said unto the woman, "What is this that you have done?"

And the woman said, weeping, "The serpent beguiled me and I did eat the fruit."

Then God said to the serpent:

Because you have done this thing, you are henceforth accursed among all living things upon earth. Upon your belly you shall crawl, both you and your kind. And you shall eat dust all of the days of your life and all that comes after you. And I will put enmity between you and the woman and between your seed and all that shall come out of you and her seed. Her seed shall bruise and crush you and you shall lie in wait to bruise her heel.

The serpent threw a stone looked at the Lord upon hearing his fate and went from out of His presence to be the eternal foe of man, but the Lord did warn him that there will be someone who will arise to defeat his evilness and redeem man's sins and paradise would be restored to him again.

In the meantime God turned to Eve and said:

Because of what you have done, you shall have many griefs and sorrows. Your children will be born to you in great sorrow and anguish. Because you loved your husband so much, in him shall you turn for strength and refuge and he shall rule over you.

He turned to Adam and said:

Because you listened to your wife's voice and ate the fruit of the Tree which I forbade you not to, cursed shall be the ground for your sake. Thorns and thistles shall it bring forth for you, and weeds be the fruits of your labor and you shall eat the herbs that springs from them. In toil and in weariness and the sweat of your brow shall you labor for bread all the days of your life until your body lies down in death and be turned again into dust where you came from in the beginning. For dust thou art and unto dust shalt thou return.

And Adam and Eve, smitten to the soul fled away from the presence of the Lord into the night and returned to the darkness of their hiding place in the Garden.

God was grieved to the heart also by these events and said to Himself:

Behold, this man has become like one of us. Although it brought him no peace, he has now attained the knowledge of good and evil. He is as if he is now divine. But now because of pride and disobedience, he may sin again and go back and pluck the fruit of the Tree of Life and live forever in shame and grief. I must not allow this to happen. He must be punished.

Because of God's great love for His two children whom He had created, it was never His intention to utterly leave them alone and abandon them completely, but He decided that they must leave their home in paradise and live in a place where there can be no peace and love except the love that they desired of Him which could bring them to love each other and bring them solace and obedience during their bitter banishment.

In the darkness that is before the dawn, they awoke and found themselves aggrieved with much sorrow. They arose and saw two cherubims from heaven armed with flaming swords and whose eyes were like flames, and they were too unbearable for Adam and Eve to look into.

They fled from the cherubims, stricken with dread, cold and anguish, and came through chasms of sea-like gold of the sun as it rose on the river that flowed beyond the Garden. The river, falling in foam and with the sound of thunder from height to height shuddered them. The vast circuit of the earth with dense and enormous forests, parched sand, checkered ice-capped mountains and great rivers and oceans was spread out beneath them.

With great haste, they went down out of Eden and did not stop to rest nor dare to look back. Night fell. It was cold and dark and they were alone.

At the east of paradise, God set the cherubims with flaming swords to guard the entrances and to turn back everyone who sought entry and to guard the way to the Tree of Life.

Wow!

Five

Let There Be Light . . .

No one could tell this tale like Miss White. This became Miss White's lie because she could tell it so well. I clung to every word she said and at times I felt as if I were right there with Adam and Eve in Eden. I really liked the part about the snake, but my mind kept harking back to the parentage portion of the story.

May and I arrived in urban Massachusetts on a sticky summer day following a long and adventurous bus ride from the orphanage in North Carolina. This ride was an additional spark which triggered my urges of curiosity and examination.

As the bus rumbled northward, I completed a quick on-the-spot curriculum in social dynamics amongst the hurly-burly Negro mothers and their multitude of snotty-nosed children of almost equal ages who sat in the back of the bus with us. One little old fat, loud-mouth, cry-baby, kinky-headed boy always accidently found my foot in his path as he ran up and down the aisle which sent him tumbling and sprawling into the back of seats and arm rests.

I paid careful attention to their discipline, clothing, speech, smartness, dumbness, manners, hygiene, fatness, snoring, blackness, cuteness, ugliness, and their chicken sandwiches. At every rest stop, they all got off and the bus driver was always trying to find one of their kids who was last seen going into the bathroom.

When we could sit anywhere on the bus as we reached the "north" in Washington, D.C., I exchanged seats and moved to the two seats just behind the driver. Wow! This was really fascinating. I examined every tree and rock along the highway; counted every telephone pole that whizzed by; recorded every license plate on cars and trucks; read every sign and billboard; gawked at the size of the buildings; held my breath through every tunnel; and nearly wet my pants crossing every bridge. May slept through all of this excitement. She was 14 years old, I was 12.

With all of this external excitement going on in my life, my Gemini mind was also preoccupied. The overriding emotion was fear. Fear!

But what was I afraid of? I even asked myself what is fear? It clearly was not just the absence of any courage. I had courage, and plenty of it. Nor was it contingent upon any impending danger.

I had it all figured out by the time we arrived. It was a reverential awe for my mythical parents which incubated in me since Adam and Eve–first Parents. I asked myself, "Would I be worthy as their son? Would they like me? Would they give me things that I asked for like new shoes and underwear, toothbrushes, and socks? I don't have anything for them. What would they think of me?"

I had deified them, and so I was awed in a divination for them which almost approximated my fear of God.

Alas! We arrived at our parents' home. "They're here," was the shout from the first floor of a building that was built and aged with the city of Worcester. I greeted my sisters and brothers and they introduced themselves:

I'm your sister Roseanne.
I'm Thomas.
I'm Paul.
I'm Peter.
I'm Linda.
I'm James.

"Andrew is in the hospital, and Mark is down the street playing."

"Hey, he looks just like daddy."

"Sure do. He looks more like you James."

"What?"

The lady sitting on the couch with her eyes pointed towards the floor murmuring, "Lord, all my chilluns don' come home," was my mother. May ran and hugged her. I stood there mummified. She walked towards me and without looking me in the face put her arms around me and cried, "My son Charlie."

I received her hug and tears with my arms glued to my sides. The glazed eyes were pointed to some place else—not here. The warm and crimson sanguinity I had anticipated reverted to ice-blue.

I looked around for my father. He was not there. I was told that my mother and father hadn't been together for many years, but he still lived in the city.

I was shown to my room behind the curtain where I would sleep. I sat on the edge of the bed in a semi-conscious state pondering if I should unpack or run away. I did not want to be there and I retreated back to my "paradise" under the front porch at the orphanage.

I made every attempt to function as a part of the family. My sisters and brothers did their part also, especially Linda and Peter. Linda was the one of the brood which immediately captured my thought train. She was a free thinker and was considered to be very close to daddy. James considered himself to be God's creative epitome of beauty. He was even called "Beauty"—after the dog. This caused a tug of war between he and Paul who captured the heart of any girl he met. Roseanne was Miss Society.

Time passed as I accepted my place in the family which, at best, was an adjunct position. I tried to reconcile my feelings with my mother on several occasions, but each time I tried, I reverted back to the "initial" hug that she gave me when we met for the first time: ice-blue, and the way she called me "Charlie."

The fact is, I did not know her and she did not know me. I became enraged and felt a deep sense of betrayal when I met her. A question arose in my mind: "How did my sister May and I get into the orphanage when I had so many other brothers and sisters, and a mother and a father?"

Several explanations were offered. They ranged from her mental capacities to her marriage to my father who worked in a junk yard to eke out a living and who deserted her and the children after I was born.

I contented myself with the fact that she was my mother by birth and amid the cares of raising a goodly brood of brothers and sisters on a scant allowance of education, love, and public assistance, she did the best she could.

I was willing to forgive the circumstances and let the lies

neutralize each other. I knew, however, from the start that there was a great educational gap between us, and the question of any maternal love from her would continually be debated.

Early one Saturday morning in August, Linda came to the house and said, "C'mon Charlie I want to show you something."

She didn't say where we were going or what we would see. I didn't ask because I was always thrilled to see her and to be with her. We walked to the produce distribution section of the city where a lot of Greeks, Italians, and Polish merchants conducted their businesses. As we walked through this section of town, she seemed to know each of the workers and merchants in the area as they all yelled their nasal New England "Good mornings" at her.

We stopped at the entrance of a coffee shop with a long counter with stools where several men were seated arguing the merits and demerits of the Red Sox.

Sitting off to the right of the counter was a man with his back towards the door sipping coffee and reading a book. Linda paused for a second then skipped up behind him and tapped him on his shoulder saying, "Hi daddy, look who I brought you."

He turned and looked right through me. His eyes were blood-red, his face was furrowed with the lines of a man who had carried many burdens. His complexion was a mixture of half-tones of red, burnt copper, and coffee. His semi-graying hair was combed into a slight pony-tail which accentuated his Native American, African American, Creole, and European features. His left eye lid had a slight skin covering from his forehead and was slightly lower than his right eye.

Linda looked at me and slapped me on the back and scooted out the door yelling, "Stay here, I'll be back a little later. You two get to know each other."

I stood there in my granite-like posture. Without calling me by name he growled, "Hello, how have you been?"

I thought those were the words spoken, but my mind was back in the clouds on Deedy's mattress listening to the invisible words of the two men in Biblical garb.

"All right."

My eyes did the best that they could by staying dry. My lips were burdened with the task of remaining closed. My fists were heavily taxed with remaining unclenched and still attached to the side of my body, and my feet stayed with me as I stood there before him.

After what seemed to be an eternity, I returned. I looked at him as if I were looking at myself, only several generations apart and a few wrinkles, otherwise, there I sat—my own mortality. He looked as though he had spat me out.

His disheveled khaki pants with hand-soiled pocket entrances were matched with a well-worn blue denim shirt with pockets stuffed with overflowing bric-a-brac and a dingy plaid necktie with the knot shoved to one side.

His left wrist was tucked inside his pocket where it remained as he gathered a cigarette from the counter and stuffed between his lips. As he reached for a book of matches to light the cigarette, he withdrew his left wrist from his pocket and the sight almost made me puke.

His hand was missing! It had been cut off! There were no fingers, no fist, no nails! I had never seen anything like it before and it shocked the living daylights out of me. I looked around for Linda. She had abandoned me. How could she leave me with this man with his hand missing.

My eyes had increased their dimensions by at least twice their size and were riveted on the handless arm as he reached out to touch me with his other hand. I jumped. Scared as hell, but my feet would not pick me up to leave. I wanted to run away, but I also felt that I wanted to stay. He ordered me a tuna sandwich which was his favorite. Mine too. I sat beside him eating the sandwich with the corner of my eye fixed upon the arm. We didn't have many words for each other—just a room full of thoughts.

When Linda returned after a millennium of time, she dashed a glance at my father and said, "Let's go, I want you to meet your other brother Andrew. I'm sure you'll like him."

I wasn't quite ready to go but we departed—without really leaving him. I looked back at him as we went through the door and caught a slight glimpse of a smile from him. I reciprocated. I never saw him again.

Six

And There Was Light . . .

We went to see my oldest brother Andrew who was in the State Hospital for the mentally ill. He had been there since World War Two after being wounded at Pearl Harbor, Hawaii while serving in the Navy. He was deemed to be shell-shocked and the Veteran's Administration had assigned him there to live out his life.

I immediately liked him as I was introduced to him. Linda brought him some newspapers including *The Wall Street Journal* which he insisted and a host of magazines including *The New Yorker* and *Forbes* magazine.

"This is your brother, Andrew, and Andrew, this is your brother Charlie."

When she had finished the introduction, he looked at her with a very puzzled look on his face, and repeated, "Charlie?"

We sat under the trees looking out at the lake and talked about everything including people he said were "crazy."

Four hours had passed in an instant when one of the attendants approached us to remind us that he should return to his room to receive his medicine. We said good-bye to him and returned home. I really wanted to see him again.

I had slid into an environment at home with my mother and accepted it. However, each Saturday I would visit Andrew at the hospital or he would receive a pass to come home for the weekend and I'd spend my time with him. He had his own room at the house, which he allowed no one to enter—sometimes this applied to my mother as well. He allowed me free entry whenever I wished. His room was kept immaculately clean with stacks of old newspapers and books and art objects.

We'd talk all of the time we had together, but he never called me by my name. "Here, look at this," or "Come here for a second," or "Hey did you ever..." were his ways of addressing me.

One day he came to me and said, "Here Amos, I want you to read this. This is something I've been working on for a long time—ever since I've been in the hospital. I'm sure you will enjoy it."

I looked at him and asked:

"What did you call me?"

"Amos, that's your name."

"My name is Charlie."

"Hunh Unh, your name is Amos, just like your daddy's name is Amos."

"My daddy's name is Willie."

"Daddy's real name is Amos. He named you after him."

"You got to be kidding. Well then how come I've been called Charlie all my life. I was Charlie at the orphanage. All my school records say I'm Charlie. All my friends know me as Charlie. Everybody knows me as Charlie. Everybody in the family calls me Charlie including my mother. Where did this

Charlie come from if my name is Amos?"

He looked at me hesitantly and spoke in a voice which sounded like it had an electronic quality to it, as if he were connected to some external source from which the words were coming:

> Let me say this to you. I have long discovered this; to belong to a family is to be owned by it. You trade your freedom for sustenance and belonging. I'll bet that you are very disappointed with the family, but don't let it bother you too much. Since I have lived in this "giggle factory" I have concluded that there is no relationship between people except that of the spirit. Most of the people here do not know one from the other. They respond to whomever gives them sustenance to make it beyond the next step and I bet you do too.
>
> I have found my relationship with my mother and these people who stuff me with all those narcotics and drugs to keep me humble, to be just a ring of conspirators trying to keep me under control. And so, I've made myself a spiritual family which serves me very well.

I looked at him and his words seemed to become very visible as they wrapped around me in total awe. I knew Andrew did not have a grey beard nor was enrobed in Biblical garb, but he appeared as such when he spoke those words to me. I listened. And for the first time, the word "family" took on a completely different meaning to me.

Yes, I was born into this family, tyrannized at the orphanage, and accepted the conditions of a fraternity of sisters and brothers, but was this really my family?

Sensing that he had caused a bit of a stir in me and had not completed answering my question, he continued:

I wouldn't blame you for getting upset when you hear what I'm about to tell you. I know I would be more than upset if I were you. Are you sure you want to know?

"Yes, go ahead and tell me."

Before you were born, mom gave birth to a baby boy who died right after he was born and they called him Charlie. Mom's mental health became very bad after that happened and after you were born, they put her into a mental institution and sent you and May to the orphanage and put the rest of us in foster homes and with other relatives. Thinking that you were that baby that didn't live, she told the officials that your name was Charlie at the orphanage, but daddy had put the name Amos on your birth certificate.

"**What?**" I was thrown into a tizzy, became furious and began to argue with myself. Just because I was deposited and cradled in a womb of spermatozoon and issued out via this woman, what right does any incompetent (or otherwise) person have to stamp me as so and so, when such stamping carries the consequences they do.

Here I was, longing for a family, especially a **mother**. Now I find out I had been stamped by this **woman** as a "Charlie"— a "living dead fetus."

I girded myself by the loins, sucked it all in, and looked at the material Andrew had given to me. Guess what the subject was. Adam and Eve!

We had a long discussion about it and he opened my eyes in a way no one else could have done. He began by asking me a series of simple questions:

"Do you believe in the Bible?"

"Of course I do, don't you?"

"Do you believe that everything is true in the Bible?"

I knew where he was taking me so I threw in a little bit of gibberish.

"Well not all things, but I believe that the words written in the Bible are true, and the Bible is true because they are written in it."

"Okay!, but do you believe the story about Adam and Eve is true?"

"Unh hunh."

"Well hear my story and see what you think about it." I listened:

>Once upon a time (millions of years ago) some hard driven men found a strip of rich land on the banks of the Euphrates River which flows through northern Africa on through to the Persian Gulf.
>
>They found a depression of the earth's surface about ten miles long and about a quarter of a mile wide close to the desert and they settled there.
>
>Eventually these men were able to irrigate a garden to assure them of a life of comfort.
>
>Soon, the irrigated land was overrun with human beings living on its fruits. The people cultivated the soil, tended the irrigation ditches, and submitted themselves to the rulers of the men who first settled there. The discipline was hard and strict which was necessary to keep the irrigation system in working order.

There was great need for this precious water and many quarrels followed. Because of a need for order, an upper caste was established.

Finally, most of the people found their conditions to be little more than slaves for the upper caste. Privilege and power for the few—poverty and obedience for the many. This is a common occasion when land and resources are scarce.

The people in this fruitful land looked around them and saw on the one side, a flowing river with fertile soil bearing plenty of food—while all around them was a forbidding desert. Out of its mysterious depths, there came from time to time, fierce and long-haired wanderers. Sometimes they were numerous and they would seize the fruit and the young maidens and killed the resisting men and the old women. When the invasion would end the invaders would disappear back into the desert to resume their life of vagrancy and uncertain existence, sweetened by savage independence.

Sometimes people would come hungry and wounded begging from the rich stores of Eden for bread and water. Sometimes they may have been granted refuge and welcomed to stay for a while. Or, they might have been absorbed into the body of the river-side dwellers, or returned, comforted to their desert. Perhaps a single man, perhaps five or ten. No matter. Tribal war could have driven them there.

Once a desert man who was African came to Eden. However, the man came begging first for life alone. Liberty and happiness he had left in the desert. The Ruler of this little place called Eden gave him bread and water and invited him to stay if he wished and enjoy the hospitality of the people, however he would have to fend for himself when he needed food and to obey the laws and customs of the people.

The stranger was unfitted by his desert upbringing to work in the trenches so he was left to pick up the surplus food from the fields after the harvest was gathered and eat the fruit of the trees.

Slowly he learned the language of the people. He called the birds and beasts by their proper names but many of the people were new to him so he gave them a name most suited to himself.

The vegetables and the fruits and grains were luscious and plentiful. He led an easy life but eventually became oh, so lonely and tired of his lazy unemployed solitude.

As far as the nobles were concerned, he scarcely existed. They hardly noticed him because he mostly stayed to himself. He did not try to adapt himself into the social class, nor was it offered to him. Their ways were not his ways. So he yearned for his own people.

He would lay on his back and recall the memories of the herds browsing over the wastes, of the swift tribal attacks, the strident war-cries, and of wounds he had given and received at his brothers' side.

And most of all came back to him, memories of the dark-eyed women whose dalliance had so often beguiled him during the soft silent star-lit hours under the desert skies. And when his heartache could no longer be borne, lo! A miracle happened which brought great happiness to him.

One night after he had slept heavily, he awoke to find that a woman of his own kind had wandered into the garden. He didn't know how she got there. She may have been chained or stricken as he had been by some fatal happening to her tribe. Or, it could have been that the dwellers in Eden had repelled a African attack by the fierce long-haired wanderer of the desert during the night and captured a maiden and held her.

Although he did not participate in the battle, he did experience a little pain from a gash in his left side. The Ruler of Eden had to decide what to do with her since none of the other men wanted to marry into her race. The man's heart swelled with hope, sweat poured from his body and the muscles began to throb for he saw that she was a very beautiful African woman. The man pleaded, Give her to me, I plead. Oh, please give her to me. She is bone of my bone, flesh of my flesh.

And the Ruler said, "She is yours."
"WAH LA WOO WAH... OOH WAH LA WOO!" shouted the man.

I asked Andrew, "Why was the man so happy? Was this his girlfriend or something?"

"No, but he was just happy that he had someone around him who he could spend some time with and to play with. Just like you did when you were younger. Okay?"

He continued with the story:

After the man saw that the woman had been given

to him, a smiling period began for this united couple. Their emotional and physical natures found complete satisfaction as they romped and played in the dance of life with each other. Happy days were passed which left many impressions on them to be passed on to their offsprings, and by them to their children and through generations following the other.

"What do you mean by that?" I interrupted.
"They became husband and wife and had children."
"By dancing and smiling?" I asked.
"What do you think? Are you trying to be smart or are you just that uninformed?"
"I just wanted to know. I'll try not to interrupt any more."
Andrew proceeded again:

Their tasks were light. There was little work to be found for them. Their days were given much to idle fancies. Their nights were packed with amorous joys. Many children were born and the leaders of the village had to provide clothing and food for the family.

Since they had simply been forgotten by the Ruler of the land and could do just as they pleased, the offspring soon began to pillage and destroy the belongings of other dwellers in the village. They were looked upon with fear and envious eyes by the servile class who worked in the field, the orchard, and the ditch.

Also, among this low caste of people, as in all times and climes, a certain rebellious cunningness of the serpent is developed.

So the man and woman were the objects of the villagers jealous suspicions and they plotted to bring about the downfall of these interlopers.

Now in this ancient garden, a few rare fruits were set aside to be for the sole enjoyment of the master class. They were threatened with punishment if they were caught eating the fruit from these rare trees.

But no discipline can be so severe and so strictly enforced as to prevent the furtive slave from tasting occasionally of the forbidden fruit, no matter how many times he is caught and lashed or imprisoned. And some petty theft did occur among the slaves and they didn't tell on each other. But if the stranger was caught eating thereof, he must surely suffer. So they plotted how to get rid of them.

One day a cunning slave with a malicious heart whispered to the woman that the master's decree forbidding the date palm to all the underlings of the Garden didn't really mean that much. He told her they ate the fruits all the time and if they were caught, the punishment wasn't too severe—they only got a warning or probation.

But the man who had dwelt in a disciplined land knew that even on the desert, obedience was also required of a warrior. He also had some touch of gratitude for being allowed to live there and so he turned away from the tempter.

No woman is ever more capricious than man. To her, unless she is completely broken by fear or love, all discipline is tyranny. She yields obedience freely only when desire commands. To all dwellers of the desert, both men and women, liberty was very sweet.

So the woman took of the fruit and ate it. When

the deed was done, when the risk was run, the man joined his fate with hers. He also took of the fruit and ate it.

The wrong done by the desert people was a triple one. First, there was petty theft. That might have been overlooked. Then there was disobedience. But more than the two previous crimes, it was a bold assertion of "social equality."

This was no easy matter to excuse because it had been put to all the subordinates by the master class, that they would remain in the caste of their birth.

And, whatever was reserved to the master, whether food, dress, or of the manner of doing things, must be taboo for them.

I couldn't hold back any longer, so I blurted, "Sort of like being a Negro, or a handicapped person, or a woman. Right?"
Andrew shot back:

What did you promise me about interrupting, but you're right! Everywhere the high caste said to the low caste, 'If you did thus and so, it meant that you were trying to become as one of us. That must not be, and you shall be punished severely, for it is rebellion and high treason.'

However, to the African pair, the succulent dates were sweet to the palate, but sweet also to their proud souls was the sense of a dangerous step upward toward freedom and independence which had been theirs in the desert. In the face of danger their spirits rose.

They decided to affront the law in yet another galling way. Only the upper class had the right to dress fully and fashionable. The underlings were scarcely clad, if at all. So the man and woman declared that they would no longer be confused with a slavish crowd of naked field workers.

The woman in particular had resented this indignity of dress or the lack of it. So she made garments for herself and for her man. How great was her sense of satisfaction when this pass had been accomplished—all women of fashion will readily understand this.

After a few generations of quiet enjoyment in the new role of token equality adopted by the intruders, time passed and things began to change.

The occasion to expose the rebellion which had been prepared by the intriguing slave had now come to maturity. In a doubtless show of loyal indignation, and an appreciation for working in the house close to the master, house slaves reported the disobedience of the Africans to the Master. The field slaves didn't care. They were not too fond of the Master anyway.

One day when the master passed to walk in the Garden in the cool of the day, sipping his mint julep, a house slave decided to take the matter in hand and suppress at once the insolence of those 'uppity intruders' who "did not know their place."

The Africans were lurking in the shade of the fruit trees with a few rebellious field slaves when they heard the Master's voice calling them. They knew it was vain to push the rebellion to the point of hiding their insolence. They knew somebody had squealed on them, and so they surrendered.

When summoned before the Master and questioned about the reasons for his action, the man stammered and told a white lie and an excuse saying that he thought it was unbecoming to appear before the Ruler without clothing.

He was admonished by the Ruler for supposing that nakedness was unfitting to one of his low estate. The Ruler then charged him with the outrageous presumption that he could eat of the fruit set apart so carefully for the great people of the land.

Frightened now by the Ruler, the man did the rather unmanly thing. He put the blame on the woman, saying, "I was seduced into tasting this fruit by this woman. You know how women are. You know you can't trust them. If you turn your back on them for one minute, they'll trick you into doing something you don't want to do."

His next defense was just as obnoxious as the previous one, but he had to tell the truth. It was quite frightening for him to do so because he would have to expose the rules of the game that had been played by the "good old boys club" and it was unmanly to tell the truth and make this a public disclosure, but that is what he did.

Perhaps he thought when he declared that he had eaten the fruit which the woman had given him, that forgiveness for both of them would be more readily granted because as he put it, "All men know how hard it is to bind a woman to the strict letter of the law."

The man continued, "Come now, Oh Great Ruler, you are a man just as I am. We are the ones who wield the most power. You wouldn't punish a fellow man would you? We are the ones who have to work in the fields all day long to feed them. We fight all the wars to protect them. All they do is stay home and have babies.

"You know that life is adjusted to the wants of the stronger sex. And that there are plenty of dangers to be crossed, but their stepping stones are measured by the strides of men and not of women. You made the duties of the woman to be contained within the confines of the bedroom, kitchen, etc."

The Ruler looked at him and said, "You idiot, don't you know that to feed, rescue, and protect a woman is all the same as loving her. Women wish to be loved without a why or a wherefore—not because they are beautiful, well-bred, graceful, or intelligent, but because they are themselves.

"Women do not transgress their bounds as often as men; but when they do, they go to greater lengths. So win and wear her as you will, but all of the collective reasoning of men such as yourself are not worth one sentiment of a single woman. She is my best and most delightful creation, endowed with love from her own heart and virtue and beauty from my handiwork. And as for you, she will always be one-half woman and one-half dream. So dream on you waif."

The man's final defense was to hint at changing responsibility for the act and to shift the blame to the Ruler, saying, "Don't blame me, this is the woman that thou gavest me."

But in all fairness to both man and woman, they

had not fully understood the gravity of the offense they had committed. How could they know the enormous importance of *keeping people in their places?* In the desert, all men were equal.

The Ruler with stern countenance then turned to the woman, "What is this that you have done?" he said.

She pleaded, "One of your slaves fooled me into eating the fruit." It was the truth, but an unavailing truth.

The Ruler then saw at a glance, all that had happened. He condemned the slaves who had taken part in the plot. They would suffer and their children would suffer as would their childrens' children. Their tasks were made baser and their food was made coarser.

"Wait, stop for a minute. I have a couple of questions. First of all, why was the Ruler so mean that he would punish their children, they didn't do anything wrong? Why should they have to take the blame for something that their parents did and they had nothing to do with?

"And this is my next question: Is that why we have to eat them old slimy okra and chitlins and pigs feet and tongue and chicken feet and brains? And is this kind of food really good for the soul? I can't stand them old slimy okra. Yuck!"

"Hey, some people like those things. I know some people who would kill for a bowl of chitlins. Your brother Paul is one. I used to be crazy about them myself. Later on, I'll tell you about the punishment for the children? But let me just finish with the story, then you can ask all of the stupid questions you want. Okay?"

"Okay for now," I said to myself.

And so the Ruler did not expel them from the Garden—that would be "cutting off your nose to spite your face."

"Why?" I asked.

Because a serf is property—something to own and to be controlled and chastised into obedience, not cast away. How could one be a Ruler if there was no one to be ruled? Understand?

"Unh Hunh."

However, the actual people who performed these acts had to be punished. This could not be tolerated. If permitted to remain, sedition might grow. Moreover, they were of little use as workers in the field. They were therefore ordered to return to the desert whence they had come.

Their life of ease was ended. The Ruler allowed them to keep the paltry garments they had fashioned and to take a few skins to protect them from the heat and cold they would now confront without the shelter of trees or a roof.

The frontiers of their exile were also established. Thirty, maybe even forty miles below the Garden of Eden were bitumen deposits. The men of that place had learned to purify the bitumen, to melt it into pitch which is tar and use it for caulking their boats. The red flames of these pits burned constantly. The tongues of these men flashed red in the night. The black pitch stuck to their bodies. The pitch that stuck to their rods for stirring the fires were ablaze as if they were flaming swords.

The disobedient pair were told that they could not

come any closer to the Garden than the fiery frontier.

The men with the red in their eyes were instructed to keep the man and women at a distance from the Garden.

"Were these like Negroes, or Africans with their black skins, and red eyes, and red tongues, and had spears that burned?"

"Shut up."

And so the woman gave birth with great anguish to each child for she knew her children would be born into a world of cold nights, coarse foods and be repelled at every attempt to reach again the paradise of cool shades and luscious fruits by the riverside.

And it came to pass that for the children, the story of Eden was fixed in their minds as the story of the beginnings of mankind.

The term "men" was universally used by the primitive groups as speaking of themselves. Often enough their only contact with other groups was in the contact of war.

Enemies were generally designated as 'men.' The generalization suggested by the word 'mankind,' comes later. And it was in this later development of ideas that the man became Adam, and the woman became Eve. And the pair became parents of the human race.

Tradition grew into myth. The Ruler of Eden who had so profoundly affected the fate of their forefathers became a God. Their offsprings in the new life, who claim to be the descendants of the dwellers in the Garden of the Gods, and were exiled from it, now claim to be the progenitors of all mankind.

This myth that has come down to us from the Pre-Christian ages has had much influence upon our civilization. For the most part, I think that influence has been unfortunate ever since the legend has been told to us as being the Word of God. And in many simple minds, that characterization still exists. Fears still hold the imagination of men because of the "extra beliefs" that have gathered around simple happenings to simple people thousands of years ago.

I hope you learn something from this, and I also hope you will continue your way through this odyssey you are on to uncover as much truth in knowledge that I sense you have.

"WOWee!

Andrew! In a giggle factory? Hunh Unh. This guy was heavy. I asked if he would let me keep this and maybe later on in my life I could share this with some other people.

"I was hoping you would say that. Yes, go on and take it. Do more to it than I have."

I tucked the material under my armpit and he pushed an old and tattered Bible in my hand saying: "Take this with you and read it. Somewhere in there you will find the truth. You just have to keep on searching for it."

Seven

The Least of Them . . .

I crossed the large expanse of freshly mown lawn as I exited the hospital. The campus was clumped with lots of people milling about. Some were solo, others were sitting on benches in small communities of three or four talking, laughing, singing, scratching, weeping, starring, eating, hugging, puffing, chewing, coughing, spitting, thinking, reading, planning, forgetting, touching, forgiving, kissing, listening, playing, caring, sharing, searching, praying, holding, loving one another, and all of the many other things that humans do. However, the stamp they wore read "Crazy."

I pondered, "If they are crazy, then so am I and everyone else. Andrew didn't appear to be crazy. The alcoholic father who lived next door to us who comes home and beats his wife and children each night, carried no such label. Neither did the pimps in the big cars hustling deadly drugs and the prostitutes peddling flesh and disease."

I tiptoed around these thoughts until I reached home and poured my eyes into the material Andrew had given me. I could hardly wait until the weekend so I could visit him again. At eight o'clock sharp I was there with him and we continued our talk just as we left it. I told him I wanted to know as much as he did about the Bible and particularly the Adam and Eve story.

He agreed that we would discuss the story and any other topic under the condition that I kept an open mind and did not take what he said as the gospel. I agreed.

His first comments were fundamental to my objectivity in looking at how I viewed religion and the worship of God.

He started off by saying what we were about to embark upon was a very complex subject and people have sought answers to the questions raised since time began, but . . .

I will make it as simple as I possibly can. You must begin any discussion of this sort with the fundamental belief that there are laws and principles which govern our lives and the universe—no matter whatever else you believe in.

Your confidence and your belief must be unshaken in this regard. Then you can go from there.

You can call it Spirit, or Consciousness, Light, Love, God, Lord, Master, or what have you, but you should be constantly aware of the fact that you are seeing and understanding **only** from your own point of view.

If you were anything else—a chicken, a rock, a tree or mule, and had the facility to posses a consciousness, then your belief system and understanding of things around you would be from your viewpoint as a chicken or a rock, tree, or mule.

If you don't remember anything else besides this,

I beg you to get this understanding firmly imbedded in your mind. This is the genesis (root word—genus meaning first) of all human understanding.

By the way, this Adam and Eve discussion is very germane to the topic we are discussing now. The old argument of which came first, the chicken or the egg is basic to the man and woman discussion. The term "woman" has been taught to us as being "from man." Adam told us this. This isn't altogether true. "Woman" means genus, seed, first, beginning.

Let me attempt to explain something to you which should give you something to think about when we discuss this topic in more detail later on. Okay?

"Unh Hunh."

Lets say that for any movement to take place, there must be two opposing principles operating—positive and negative. Like the two opposing ends of a battery. These two principles are in no way in conflict with each other. One cannot operate without the other. Einstein worked this out pretty well and you might want to study it for a fuller understanding of this discussion.

In our consideration of the principles of nature as they relate to the creation of man and women, it is my understanding that the two generating forces which interact with each other to form this union are male (animus dei, positive force) and female (anima mundi, from the Latin meaning passive force or **soul** of the universe which connotes into the word **see** which connotes into the planting of an **idea**). The idea of a thing represents its soul. And so the **soul** acts as a

soil for nurturing. It is just like the soil, neutral, which will nurture anything planted in it.

So I ask you the question, can you have an ear of corn without first having the seed of corn?

Can you have a chicken without an egg which is the seed, or a birth of a human without the egg of a woman? You may say okay but can that same question be reversed. It certainly can. You can easily look at an apple and the seed of an apple and ask the question—how many seeds are in this apple, as opposed to how many apples are in this seed.

To begin your inquiry by looking at the egg, cornstalk, or the apple, is reversing the question and is reflective of a conception of finitude, as opposed to infinitude, reality versus potentiality, limited versus unlimited.

Let me explain. If you believed in a world of reality, then the chicken came first. Feathers are very real, so are apples and cornstalks.

However, if you believed in a world of potentiality, then the egg came first because an egg is a potential chicken. The chicken is the "idea" which the egg will produce. And where does all production of things you see around you begin—in the mind? Right?

"Unh Hunh."

Someone had to have the idea first, and then it was produced. It is the same as being unlimited as in creativity—unbounded. Your potentials are unbounded and unlimited. But if you ate the chicken, it places a limitation on the chicken population and threatens its continual existence.

And so it raises the Creation question, did God begin this universal plan with built-in obsolescence from a limited beginning or was it unlimited?

Was the Word which started all of this reflective of a limited power or unlimited? From our human understanding of what God is—He is unlimited, omnipotent, omniscience, and omnipresence.

Can such a power produce a plan which is limited in scope and duration? I think not, so it is my belief that the seed of the woman had to precede the production of the man.

That is what creation is all about. You create first, then you produce. The Book of Genesis has God in a topsy-turvy situation. He becomes sculpturer or painter first then he becomes the artist. There is a difference between a painter and an artist.

Are you still with me?"

"Unh Hunh!"

"Now having said all of this, it is my contention that man and woman were both created simultaneously."

"Hunh! Are you contradicting yourself? You just said that woman came first."

I did? I don't recall giving you a sequence of order for their production, I just explained the principle behind their existence. If you will go back to Genesis, you will see that the Creator created the herbs of the earth, the beasts of the field, the fish of the sea, and the fowl of the air. Did the Creator make the rooster before the hen, or the bull before the heifer, or the male bee before the queen bee, or the male plant before the female plant? Think about these things. I think we've discussed quite a bit today.

He raised himself from the chair and starred out the window for a second. As he stood there, a faint glow seemed to have appeared on his face. I felt a slight bit of fright creep into my body, but it felt good.

I gazed at him for a second and my mouth flung open while gasping deeply within myself. I honestly felt a certain power that he possessed which I could not correctly recognize.

Was he...? Naw, he couldn't be.

He turned to me and said, "You'd better get home now before it gets dark. Helen will be wondering what I had done to you."

I backed out of the room without taking my eyes off of him and backhandedly turned the doorknob and opened the door still gazing at him as he shushed me home.

I couldn't wait to tell my sister, May, some of the things we said. When I told her that I didn't believe that man was created by God before He created woman, she slapped my shoulder shouting, "Charlie, don't you go around and start talking to me about some foolish thing such as that. That's blasphemy. The Bible said man was first. Woman came from the man."

Her slap created a different type of relationship between us. I looked at her and saw a great deal of similarity between her and my mother. I kept to myself during most of the week and wouldn't discuss it with anyone. My mother casted oblique glances at me when we passed or met in the house. I knew my time for living in this place was becoming limited.

I met Andrew and we sat on the bench next to the lake, and he said to me, "I must have shaken you up quite a bit last week, didn't I?"

"Unh Hunh."

"Did you tell Helen about our discussion?"

"No, but I did tell May."

"Did she think you were crazy?"

"Unh Hunh."

"Thought she would. You're thinking about leaving aren't you?"

"Yeah. I don't think I want to live in this city. I don't like it at home. I don't like it when I see you up here.

May's done gone and got herself pregnant by some man older than daddy. She is just a child herself."

"What did Helen say about it?"

"She just said that she'll keep the baby. Maybe the man will marry her. But if he doesn't, she would take her down to the welfare office and let her start getting help from the welfare department."

Andrew reached down and picked up a rock and whirled it into the lake and watched the eruption of the splash as the rock hit the water. I could tell that he was agitated. This was the first time I had seen him with such demeanor. He had always carried a placid and calm behavior whenever I saw him, even when he was excited.

We both starred at the concentric circles made by the rock in the water. I could feel him thinking just as I was that this would be her way of life. Just as those circles which radiated out from the center, there would be the same rippling effect on her life if she listened to my mother.

First, my mother being a welfare dependent, puts May on

welfare, then her children go on welfare, then her children's children go on welfare, and soon there will be a generation of welfare dependents in my family because my mother started it all.

I remembered very vividly the embarrassment I felt when my mother took us to the welfare office to register us as her dependents when we first came to Massachusetts.

I thought to myself, here I am again being controlled by some government agency. In North Carolina it was the orphanage, in Massachusetts, the welfare department. I didn't like it at all. Will I ever be free from all of this control? I'll never go on welfare that's for sure.

My brow furrowed as he touched my shoulder and said to me, "Amos, this is only the beginning. You'll feel a lot more as you get older. But carry these feelings with you wherever you go. They are healthy. And they will be a healing source for you as you begin your relations with other people. I wish you would stay. But you have to do what you think is best for you. You're how old?"

"Thirteen."

I turned to him and said, "You are my brother. And I love you. I wouldn't want to leave you."

"Love! Where did that come from?"

That was the very first time I had used it with any member of my family. It just slipped out and sat there, right between the two of us. It wasn't difficult. It wasn't hard at all. It seemed to have had an evaporating power to chase the clouds away, and I saw a calming effect take hold of him.

He asked me if I wanted to continue last week's discussion. I enthusiastically gave him my patented, "Unh Hunh" and told him that I had been reading the material and the

First Book of Genesis. We removed ourselves to his room and he sat by the window and stated that the discussion would get a bit more complicated as we moved along and he would take me slowly.

Eight

My Brethren . . .

To begin we must look at what some of the words mean in the story. The word "Adam" seems to mean "the man." It is still in the speech by the people in Tibet to mean "man." However, there is a root meaning of the word and it is "red" or "red earth."

Now, listen to me carefully, if we hold to this meaning, we have here a hint of a distinction being made to show Adam as being different from other men. Was he then, the "red man?"

Did this designation refer to some personal color characteristic, or to some racial color as we have come to know, which identified him with a race of people? I'm just putting the question to you to think about at this time. We'll explore that a little bit later.

Eve is first called merely "woman." And this designation was given to her by Adam, not God. If you are able to read the Hebrew text, she is called "Isha" or "Chavah" which means "living."

There is a God which the Buddhists worship today

called "Shiva." You should acquaint yourself a little more with these things—anyhow, let's move one.

Let's look at what has come to us as myth and ask ourselves, what is the function of myth? Is it to tell us a story about things which really happened or is it to empty reality and tell us a story based upon probability? As you look at the readings which I have given you, and study the readings in the Bible, it would not seem too unreasonable to suppose that many of the myths which have come to us are just plain folklore which have been distorted over the years by either tribal pride, superstition, error of translation, copying, and conscious changes by religious persons who made these stories fit within their own religious purposes.

As a result we have a bunch of "stuff" which is a wide variety of stories which are either impossible, improbable, without precedent or fact, and contradictory within themselves.

If you are sincere in your learning, you should go back to the beginnings and come up with some type of test or a hypothesis to see if you can arrive at some story or legend which is possible, probable, founded on precedent, and does not contradict itself.

It would be extremely difficult to do so because in our daily lives, we find ourselves carrying messages with modification to suit whatever purpose we deem necessary. Even though the message may be true in all respects in it's origin. The use and its application, be it the timing in order to make a point; the manner—to show respect; or whatever reason, we use the message to suit our own purpose.

Many of these myths or stories contain the most fantastic and abhorrent details. If you strongly believed in the existence of a Creator, or a God, or a Benevolent Being, then when these details are tested against any possibility or contradiction, you will have great difficulties in making them fit just as when you feel strongly for a person be it trust, love, respect or otherwise.

If you received a message which reported contrary information, you become awed with disbelief or agitation and exclaim: 'how could it be so, this couldn't have been the case,' when it could very well have been the case. So what do we do? We resort to the same mechanisms as the ancients—we interpret or allegorize it for our own purposes. This happens sometimes even when we put the message or the story to the test of possibility or contradiction and find out that it is true in origin.

When interpretations of these stories have been repeated to us often enough and long enough, they are thought to be the last word on the subject and human reason can apply a great deal of perplexing "stuff" to a group of vanishing people or who no longer exist.

But, when your intellect finds itself unable to accept these myths or messages they should become the subject of your most careful examination. This should apply to all subjects and beliefs including religion no matter how fervid your religious feelings are.

And so to get back to our discussion, we really don't know exactly how and in what form the Hebrew exiles first found the second and third chapters of Genesis. It would be a vain attempt to try to fix the time and place of the evolution of the beginning of our civilization. It becomes more confusing when you read John 1:6-11 especially verse ten which states that: 'He (John) was in the world, and the world was made by him, and the world knew him not.' This contradicts Genesis very noticeably.

So, we must be content to point out the reasonableness and possibilities to show how the final form of the story took place. But in attempting to do so, I want to emphasize that we do not know with confidence that any single word or phrase that we now read whether in Hebrew, Greek, Swahili, or Chaucerian English, gives us the exact thoughts of those who first told the story. Just as you would not have knowledge of the exact thoughts of the person who brought you a message that your brother is dead, or your house is on fire. They could both very well be true, but the messenger could be a fireman, or an arsonist; a doctor, or a murderer.

Nine

Ye Shall Know . . .

I have given you some basic rules we will follow in our discussions and I think it would be beneficial at our next meeting for you to look at my reconstructed "story" and test some of the principal assumptions I have presented and see if you can peep through the veil of tradition and ignorance covering the actual sets of events. I want you to look behind these events to test my assumptions which include the following:

1. Behind the words Deity, Ruler, Master, or God, we have, in fact, a ruling class over a servile caste.
2. Behind Adam and Eve who were designated as the first pair of the human race, we have people who because of some misfortunes entering into a place which is governed by a ruling class.
3. Behind the serpent we have a servile class—some were mischief-makers who urged the pair to disobey the command of the Ruler.
4. Behind the words referring to a fruit reserved for the ruling class for their own enjoyment, we have a prohibition to eat that which is forbidden because it would in-

volve a knowledge of good and evil and eternal life.
5. The punishment given to the pair for their disobedience was to thrust them back into the desert from whence they had come.
6. And the offending servants were punished by making their labor harsher and their food baser, but were kept within the garden because of their value as laborers.

He paused and said, " You've got a lot to do until I see you again. I'm a bit worn out so I must lie down for awhile and rest."

Although it was a long and gruesome session, I still did not want to leave, but as I sat there on the floor for just a few minutes in my own thoughts, Andrew was on the bed already snoring. I looked at his very peaceful face and watched the rise and fall of his chest as he breathed in and exhaled every breath heavily and exhaustively. I returned home and went right to my room and drifted off into a place that was very distant from Worcester.

Andrew came home with a weekend pass the next Friday and I was thrilled to go the hospital with my mother to bring him home and to see him. As we were filling out the forms for his release, I asked the attendant if it was possible for him to spend longer periods of time at home. The attendant pulled me aside and told me that Andrew, in his opinion, had no business there in the first place. Surely he could spend more time at home, it only required someone in the family to sign him out.

I asked my mother why couldn't she sign him out to come home more often. She said, "Aw, I don't wanna be foolin wit no Andrew. I got 'nough worryin wit'out havin, to botha wit him." I snapped a look of defiance at her, and if it hadn't been for the strong discipline which was instilled in me at the orphanage—to respect older people, never to be sassy or a smart-alick—I would have lit into her without restraint. I stormed out of the building and joined Andrew and I suggested that we walk home together.

When we arrived at home, I asked my brother Peter if he could sign for Andrew to come home. He said that he used to do it, and sometimes Andrew would come home and stay for weeks at a time, but somehow the two of them, Andrew and my mother, sort of rubbed each other the wrong way.

Peter was the only other brother I felt close to but not in a brotherly sense. He always seemed to listen to me if I had any questions about the family.

He and Linda would offer to take me places with them, either to the movies on Sundays or they would recommend places for me to go to meet other boys and girls my age. He was sort of like a father to me. I respected him a lot.

Roseanne, whose mouth was as big as the ocean and a brain as spacious as a whale, was married to a successful builder and had assumed a pseudo **nouveau-riche** superficial lifestyle. She thought she was very beautiful and used her beauty as currency. Her devoted husband worked his butt off to give her everything she wanted. I'd spend time at her house when I wanted to get away and feel good in comfortable surroundings.

James was married with two boys and was the owner of two laundries and a laundromat. I hung around him because I wanted to get out of the house and ride around with him and be shown off as his younger brother. This relationship grew into a more substantive one as we grew older. I actually grew to like him.

Paul and Thomas were like yesterday's headlines—every time

something happened to them, you read or heard about it. Mark was a nonentity to me. He was very close to mother and I had nothing much to say to him. I knew the dynamics of the relationships between my brothers and my mother included a closeness between Mark, my mother, and James. The other boys were outside of this trinity.

We didn't spend much time talking about our discussions the weekend Andrew was home. He spent most of his time to himself in his room reading the stack of newspapers he brought with him. Very often I'd hear my mother admonish him for doing something she felt was intolerable to her. I saw one incident he did which I thought was innocuous, but he was rebuked by her for doing it.

She had completed cooking the Sunday dinner, (she actually cooked our Sunday meal on Saturday and we'd just warm it on Sundays because her religion said she should not cook or do other chores on the Sabbath) when she heard Andrew in the kitchen raising the lid to one of the pots on the stove, she yelled, "All right Andrew, if you don't git otta dat kitchin, I'm gonna called dem people up dere and have dem come 'n pick you up 'n take you back dere."

The distance between us began to widen each day and I silently began to make my plans to leave. I thought the orphanage was bad, this was even worse.

The orphanage began to look like a paradise compared to this. I had developed some coping skills to learn to put up with the tyranny of Peay and how to avoid the atrocities of the rest of the children. At least I had Shoe and Deedy and Booster and Henry and Modestine and Joe Lewis and of course, Leyla, all of whom I missed very much. We were all inmates in this place since Baby Cottage and we knew each other through and through right down to each others' heartbeat. I missed them. They were my brothers and sisters.

While thinking about these things, I wanted to write to them and tell them how much I missed them and what had happened to me since I left them. I sent them pictures and little boxes of junk I thought each one would enjoy.

I never received a reply from any of them. I'm not sure they even received their gifts because Mr. Peay opened the mail and would either take the contents for himself or just wouldn't give it to you—depending upon how well we had been behaving.

Receiving mail at the orphanage was one of the greatest joys and pleasures we had. I think I received two pieces of mail during my entire time there. One piece was from the Kellogg company which sent me a little plastic soldier after I had sent them a coupon from a box of cereal. Mr. Peay would not let me receive it because I had done something wrong. I can't recall what it was. It could have been because I had "cussed somebody out."

When the mail came, he kept the package for about three days before calling me to receive it. All of the children (especially May) were just as anxious as I was to see what it was since this was the first piece of mail I had ever received. I told her that whatever it was we would share it. He finally called me and opened it and showed me the gift and my eyes lit up.

However, he placed the gift on the floor and ground it into little pieces with his foot while stating with a guerilla grin on his face, "Until you learn how to behave, you ain't never gonna git nothing."

My tears were uncontrollable as I became enraged with anger, not sorrow. I didn't like this feeling because it blotted out too many thoughts that I always carried with me. The most important one was to make the best out of everything I did and to keep my vision on those two men I saw in the clouds in Biblical clothing.

The next experience was more devastating. This was due to the fact that I had been searching and asking every person I met if they knew or heard of any people named "Broomfield."

One day a man was hired to work with the big boys at the orphanage. He was from Baltimore, Maryland. I asked him the same question as with all the others and he said to me, "Sure, I used to know a guy by the name of Broomfield."

"What! You do? Tell me about him. Where is he? How can I find him?"

"The last thing I remember, he used to work with us in a sawmill. He was from up north somewhere. But I don't know what happened to that guy."

"What was he like? What did he look like? Did he look like me? What color was he? Was he my complexion? Did he have any children? Was he my daddy?"

"I can't remember too much about him. He used to keep to himself all the time. I know that much. That was some time ago maybe five or six years ago. And I vaguely remember that something was wrong with his hand."

"What was his name?"

"His name was Amos. We called him Willie."

Great Googly Woogly!

I have found my parents. I threw the shovel into the ditch where we had been working in mud up to our waist trying to drain the cesspool, and ran to find May—still dripping and smelling like the cesspool.

She was in the laundry room hanging up freshly washed sheets and towels when I burst through the rows of wet sheets yelling, "May, May, I don' found daddy. I know where he is. Mr. Bullock told me that he lives in Baltimore."

I grabbed her and held her real tight and we stayed there yelling and crying until Miss White came over and popped me on the head saying, "Nigga git outta heah. Look at whut you don' did wit dese sheets."

I left there and went straight to my locker and took out a piece of paper to write a letter. It began:

> *Dear Daddy:*
> *How are you? I am fine. This letter is from your son Charlie and your daughter May.*
> *We miss you very much. Please come and visit us soon and take us home so we can live with you.*
>
> *Sincerely,*
>
> *Charlie and May.*

I closed the envelop and addressed it:
Mr. Willie Broomfield
Baltimore, Maryland

I borrowed a stamp from Joe Lewis and mailed it. We were all very excited. I could now boast to them that I also had parents. And they were just as happy as I.

Weeks passed and there was no reply to my letter. May asked me everyday if I thought he would write to us. I always told her that God is looking after us and we didn't have to worry.

One day Mr. Peay came with the mail. I trembled from

head to foot. I reached for the letter as he handed it to me with his orangutan grin.

I looked at the envelope and became very numb; it was the letter that I had sent returned to me stamped: "**RETURN TO SENDER, ADDRESS UNKNOWN.**"

I tore the letter into little pieces as my head felt as if it would explode. I ran to the locker room and sat in a corner and Booster said to me, "Charlie, don't cry, we all love you, you're just like one of us. Someday, you'll be leaving this place."

I couldn't bear to tell May. I never did. I told her that maybe the letter had gotten lost in the mail. But I was sure that we would be hearing something soon. We never did. The incident passed and I'm certain May knew that I didn't tell her the truth about the letter. She never told me.

Ten

The Truth . . .

*I*t had been nearly two weeks since we had our last discussion and I was eager to get back into it. I had been reading the Book of Genesis and also studying the material from Andrew, and I was fully prepared to sink my wits right into it. We began by analyzing the Book chapter by chapter.

Andrew commented that it was not known when the Book was written. However, he said that it does appear that the final writing was written between 300 B.C. and 150 B.C. from three different rather loosely intertwined stories.

The oldest of these stories is the Jahvist which was written around 850 B.C. The person who wrote the second version known as the Elohist story sometime around 650 B.C. adapted his story to it, and the person who wrote the third version known as the Priestly story around 450 B.C. adapted both of them.

As he talked, his facial expression suddenly changed as he sank into a seemingly professorial demeanor. His voice became sonorous. His hands and arms became animated, and he packed every pause with a great deal of feeling.

I listened hungrily to him as I assumed another feeling—not as a brother but as a student. I was a student who took away from these discussions what was brought to them, i.e., great feelings of exhilaration and enthusiasm—a student who was sent away stepping lightly, and with a racing heart.

This, to me, was my learning process with him. It wasn't difficult. It wasn't so much as for him to bestow facts upon me as it was to impart a feeling. This, Andrew certainly did. I felt that I had learned something every time I left him, albeit the facts were there, but they took second tier.

He raised himself from the seat in which he was sitting and walked to the window and leaned against the edge of its frame resting his head against it—back against the wall; arms crossed and locked against his chest; and without looking at me, or anything else but the ceiling, he spoke:

Amos, (he was the only person to call me this) before we go any further, and I'm sure you can understand what I'm about to say so I'll freely say it to you. Since I've been in this place, I've evolved into a new way of thinking. It is so new that it is really quite ancient.

Plato tapped into it, so did Socrates and Pythagoras and Pericles and Plotinus. I've glazed it with my thoughts and has supped with Pohaku over it for the last 12-15 years.

Pohaku is my neighbor across the hallway who first introduced me to this. He's, by the way, from Concord and I guess he was bitten by the Emersonian virus which landed him in this place.

His son is the director of the United States Secret Services, and it was, in his judgement, a matter of national security that he be placed in here rather than running loose with his battery of thoughts. He was too dangerous.

One good thing about this place which I like very much is, in here, society has given us complete license to think and speak and act just as we please. Now what better paradise can a person find themselves in considering the alternatives.

This is our Garden of Eden, and each of us here has eaten not one bite of the apple—we ate the whole Tree.

I was drawn into Pohaku's embrace as I noticed his ability to divide society into two parts—one of darkness and one of light. I recalled, "And the Lord God divided the light from the darkness." His ease of ability to bridge the gulf of time with imagination also intrigued me. His never ending thirst for learning was never quenched.

I joined him in his belief that it doesn't make much difference what a person studied because all knowledge is related and the person who studies anything and if he kept at it, became learned. Each year he embarks upon a different learning endeavor.

As far as I know, Pohaku is the only living person who knows how many acorns that tree (pointing to the acorn tree outside his window) produced last year—he counted them. It may have been **50,000** or **150,000**, he knows because he studied them. Yet people think he's crazy.

He has surpassed the old cliche world of worn out rhetoric and hypocrisy and has built one upon what he calls **"Autonomic Thought" (AT)** which is a coefficient of New Thought as opposed to **"Supplanted Thought" (ST)** or Second Hand Thought.

Let me explain what the two entail. **AT** is made up of thoughts you, yourself think. The other kind is given to you by jobbers, you know, teachers and preachers and writers and movie makers and reporters, people of that sort.

As I said before, the distinguishing thing about **AT** and the beauty of it, is its antiquity.

By necessity it has to be older than **ST**. But all genuine **AT** is true for the person who thinks it. It only turns sour and becomes wrong when it is not used, or when the owner of it forces someone else to accept it. Then it becomes **ST**.

All of **AT** is revelation. **AT** revelations are like half soles on your shoes of stupidity and their heels are made up of greed. But like your shoes, they too become worn out and useless and **AT** equips you to discard them.

Very often you are going to be inspired by others to think, as I'm sure I have been with you, but in your heart, keep the **AT**, and let the person, the incident, the book, merely remind you that it is already yours.

You'll find that **AT** is always simple. **ST** is abstruse, complex, patched, peculiar, costly, and most importantly, it is passed out to be accepted—not to be understood.

Let me give you an example. We have the commandment: 'Thou shalt not make unto thyself any graven image.' This is **ST** of the first order. First, the man who originally said it may have known what it meant (remember our discussion about the messenger), but it surely has nothing to do with us now. But that does not keep us from piously repeating it over and over, and to make our children memorize it.

We have people who model clay, who wax and carve statutes and we respect them for their artistry. This commandment is foolishly founded on the fallacy that graven images are gods. It does not add anything to our happiness, nor does it shape our conduct, or influence our habits. Everybody knows and admits of its futility, yet it still sits there in our theological system. **ST** always speaks in a loud voice saying this is the only thing that is genuine, all of the others are spurious and dangerous.

Now on the other hand, we are told to 'be gentle and keep our voices low.' This is **AT**. We can only become at one with ourselves and with our inner consciousness or our God through silence. God is found in the silence, not in the whirlwind.

The reason Job had such difficulty hearing God, is because God reportedly spoke to him out of the whirlwind. **AT** says take this only as it appeals to you as your own. Accept it all, or in part, or reject it all, but in any event, do not believe it merely because I say so.

AT is founded on the laws of your **own nature**, and it says to you, '**Know thyself. Know who you are.**' **ST** is founded on authority and it says **"Obey."**

AT offers you no promises of paradise or eternal bliss if you accept it; nor does it threaten you with everlasting hell if you don't. All it offers is unending work, constant effort, new difficulties and beyond each success there is a new trial.

Its only satisfactions are that you are allowing your life to unfold itself according to its own nature. And we'll talk about these laws as they pertain to Adam and Eve in more detail later on.

However, these laws are divine, therefore making you divine just as much as you allow yourself to be possessed by your own being, not someone else.

AT allows this current of divinity to flow through you unobstructed. **ST** offers no plan for elimination. It tends to congest, inflame, disease, stagnate, and disintegrate.

AT holds all things lightly, gently, easily—even thought itself. It works for health, happiness and well-being both now and forever. It does not believe in violence, force, coercion or resentment because all of these things will just turn about and act upon yourself. It has faith that all men if not interfered with by other men will eventually evolve into **AT** and do what is best and right and beautiful and true.

ST's chief proclamation has always been that it is a good police system.

AT says you should know thyself and that's enough. **AT** is free thought and cannot be forced upon us.

What do you think? Make any sense to you?

"Yes siree. All kinds of sense and I think I'll continue to peer into this subject."

Andrew instantly snapped back to the discussion we had

begun, but his appearance was quite different. Now he looked at me when he spoke instead of the ceiling, and his voice was mixed with moisture and had a more earthly pitch to it. Cocking his head to one side, and with a burst of energy, he continued:

You know it seems to me that the Adam and Eve story must have given the writers some tremendous headaches in their efforts to mesh these three stories. Even you can readily see that there is a lack of continuity there.

Just a quick glance of the second chapter of Genesis states that only one tree is prohibited. Then we go to the third chapters in verses 22-24 and two trees are prohibited.

I do believe that this is a sloppy commingling of two distinct stories—a creative story and a paradise story. If you will notice the paradise story begins with verse 8 of the second chapter when the Lord God **planted** a garden. Planting is something that a God doesn't do. It's a duty of humans to plant. God creates.

Moreover, the word "written" as we now use it cannot actually be applied to a group of illiterate people who transmitted their traditions orally.

The Hebrews did not start writing before they went into Egypt, but when they left they had accumulated enough of an alphabet that they could engrave at least thirteen commandments on stone, so we are told. We even argue about the number of commandments. Were there thirteen or were there ten? If there were thirteen what happened to the other three? If they were broken, then they must have had frail underpinnings if they could be broken even before they were executed; and then neither can we find surety in the worn out "written in stone" cliche.

He was amusing and I was really impressed with his intimate knowledge of the history of the Bible and so I delved deeper into the subject myself and asked him, "Why are there so many interpretations of this one story?"

He stated, "I don't know but I can think of at least four or five different reasons myself. Want to hear them?"

"Yes, of course. Go right ahead."

First of all I think it was an obedience test. This test could have been done in one of several ways. It could have involved Adam's active or passive behavior. For instance, Adam could have been ordered to walk two miles a day for two days—no more and no less.

If he walked one mile or three miles on a particular day, he would have been disobedient and punished because he had used his powers of discernment, as well as his disregard of walking the decreed daily distance, even though the actual miles in two days would have totalled evenly.

Once again, and I stated it in one of my assumptions, that the act which he disobeyed carried with it the obtaining of some knowledge. This knowledge could have been just the discovery by Adam that he **could** disobey a divine command.

It could also be that the knowledge gained was the discovery of a sexual relation.

"Really," I exclaimed. "How could that be?"

I'm not just talking about sexual intercourse. I'm saying that it opens the question as to whether God had other humans in His original plan.

If Adam and Eve were to have children, as you well know, men and women are physically organized for producing "each unto its own kind," remember. So I ask, how else would they have had children? How did the animals have off-springs when God told them to be "fruitful and multiply?" Did not Adam watch them "go at it?"

"Wow, I never thought about it."

Just one more for you to think about. It could very well be that the story represented the humans' efforts to establish a beginning. It established an ethical standard with the idea of good and evil. I'll get into that in more detail later on.

Oh yes, the serpent. Many simple minds, myself included at one time believed the story as it was told to us as being true in all respects. I then moved from that view to the belief that the serpent was a figure of speech representing two things—an **evil being** striving to destroy the purposes of the Creator, or a **principle of evil**.

It still bothers my mind, if you hold to this view, why would an evil being or principle be included in a divine plan by the Creator in the first place.

He paused, "Had enough?"

"Hunh Unh. Tell me more about the serpent. I heard it had something to do with sex."

"It had more than to do with sex although there were some sexual allusions in my presentation to you. We'll get into that later. Okay."

"Well all right as long as you don't forget about the sex part."

"I promise you I won't. So don't go getting yourself all worked up."

"Okay, but you promised."

Shut up and listen. As I said earlier, the serpent is seen by some as representing an evil principle in the woman. I think it is just a bunch of crap though. However, if we follow this conception, we will see that it is not consistent with the separate curses laid upon Adam and Eve on the one hand, and the serpent on the other.

Furthermore, it is not consistent with the enmity which was declared between the seed of the serpent and the seed of the woman.

"I don't understand."

Okay. To curse a principle and to deal with the children of a principle is just simply nonsense. If you recall, both the seed of the serpent and the seed of the woman are given similar punishment based upon a principle of evil which the **woman** represents. This is not at all fair to the serpent. Do you understand?

"Unh Hunh. Go ahead."

Okay. So we also have to deal with the theory that the serpent represents a demon—an evil being. If this was the case, then the punishment given to the woman is unfair. And, it is an insult to the mind of any rational human being to believe that a real serpent or any other animal spoke to Eve.

I reject it on the grounds of insufficient evidence and of maximum improbability. And the punishment itself further insults the mind—'upon thy belly shalt thou crawl.'

Tell me, how did he get around before? Did not God also make all creeping things. Were these creeping things' carrying a curse before Adam and Eve disobeyed. God did look upon all that He created and saw that it was 'good.'

Look up the word 'crawl' and see what it tells you.

"Crawl - to creep, methods of moving like reptiles or worms."

Now look up "creep."

"Creep - to move with the body on or close to the ground, as a reptile."

Now this child's talk is supposed to be God talking? Are we then to suppose that this language was deliberately used by God to confuse the minds of His creations and making them victims of mass ignorance and contending theories of interpretation?

I could go on and on about the different serpent theories, but you are anxious to get to the sex part. It might not be as intriguing as you expect.

"Just go on and tell me."

The serpent has long played a large part in the superstitions of many people. His unusual shape; his sinuous locomotion; his flicking tongue; his perfect silence; his stealthy entrance into dark caves, bed chambers, and his mortal stroke have all contributed to these fears and superstitions. It has also been the subject and idol in ancient practices of serpent worship and phallic worship.

"What's that, phallic worship?"
"Its penis worship."
"What? Penis worship? What's that all about? You mean to tell me that people used to worship another person's penis? How did they do that? You think somebody would have worshipped my penis? Just think! Me . . . Penis God . . . Omni-Potent . . . Serendipitous Ruler of the Night . . . Boastful and Belligerent Machiavellian . . . Arbiter of the Day. Wow!"

He chuckled and said:

My, you have a keen imagination, but I doubt it and shut up so I can tell you something more. It was an ancient form of pagan worship which was practiced by primitive (and not so primitive) people to worship and deify the reproductive organs of humans.

This is the oldest of any religion or belief now known. It predates the Christian era by many centuries. It does not worship just the male organ, but female also.

There is a "Secret Museum" in Naples, Italy which contains relics of ancient idols shaped in the form of the reproductive organs of males and females. These relics are made of stone, metal, pottery, ivory and gold, varying in all sizes from charms which can be worn about the neck to statues of gigantic size.

In some countries, the male organ was considered all powerful, in another it would be that of the female. In Ireland there are carved figures representing the female organ in entrances to churches, and in Egypt a King erected a temple using the male organs as pillars.

In Japan there are various little gods and some of them are made to imitate the male organ. They are prayed over by barren women seeking to give childbirth.

At Kamakura, there is a large boulder which is a perfect representation of the female organs. Some say it was the work of nature, others say it was the work of some pagan artist. Barren women go there and kneel and pray and make offerings including money and themselves to the priests thinking it will make them fertile.

At one time it was a custom for virgins to sacrifice their virginity to a phallic idol before marriage in order to prevent sterility.

This may be of interest to you. Have you seen people put horseshoes over the entrances to their doorways?"

"Yes I have. We used to do that in the orphanage. It was supposed to bring you good luck."

"Good luck? I doubt it! This is a carry-over from the practices of pagan worship. It was a universal practice of the Arabs of Northern Africa to nail up in front of their tents, over their doors, the genital organs of cows, mares or she-camels to keep the witches away."

"**Holy Cow!** Is that where this expression came from? I blurted."

I don't know, but when it became impossible to get one of these, they made a rude drawing of the same as a substitute. Some artists were better than others and so they eventually assumed various shapes, but they always approximated the genitals.

It finally took the shape of a horseshoe, and when the original meaning of this sign had been forgotten, the horseshoe became the symbol. The Hebrews, the early Christians, and Moslems attacked this practice with much zeal and many prejudices were formed, not only to the phallic idols, but to the least exposure of the sexual organs.

Recall: 'Thou shall not make unto thee any graven images?' Anyhow, this attack against phallic worship was so intensified that the Moslems were not just satisfied with covering the female sexual organs, but the women are now wholly secluded from public observation. Even their faces must be concealed.

We closed this session when Andrew was summoned for dinner by his neighbor across the hallway. He said we would continue our discussion concerning the forbidden fruit and what it may have represented.

My head was reeling from this session but I was anxious and excited with anticipation for the next one.

Eleven

From Dust Thou Came . . .

I scampered home and walked into an argument between May and my mother. It was concerning a man that May had been seeing and whom my mother had also been dating. "If you'd steyed away from him yo wudn't of gotten yo'sef knocked up. Jes stey 'way frum my mens," I heard mother say to her.

"Me stay away from them? You better tell them to stay away from me. That man forced me to have sex with him. All of these men you bring around here, all of them tries to mess with me, especially them old soldiers you be bringing in here."

My mother looked at me and yelled, "Where you been? I bet you been up dere at dat hospital talk'n dat ole crazy stuff 'bout God wit Andrew. I don't wont you bringin' dat stuff in heah."

Once again I restrained from responding to her so I dismissed her from my mind and began to make plans for my departure.

As I contemplated on leaving, my mind harked back to the days I spent in North Carolina when I used to run away from the orphanage. I thought about the difficult times I went through to leave there and how wonderful it would be for us to be with our parents but to come to something like this! Hunh Unh. No way would I stay there.

I recalled quite vividly the first time I ran away. Modestine and I developed our scheme to escape. It happened one day when the schoolday was over and the city buses which transported the children who lived in the city and attended the public school in the county, was leaving. We boarded the city bus instead of the "yellow canary" which we normally rode to take us back to the orphanage.

Modestine said he was going to his sister's house and would ask her if we could stay with her. When the bus arrived in the city, we got off near a spot which he said he recognized and his sister lived nearby.

We walked in the direction he felt he was familiar with. We walked . . . and walked . . . and walked . . . and walked . . . and then we walked some more. My feet had begun to hurt and I began to notice that several of the stores and houses were starting to look familiar, and besides, it was getting dark.

I asked Modestine where did his sister live. He said he thought she lived on 13th Street right off Woodland Avenue in the section of the city called Dreamland. I asked him what was the address. He said he didn't know the house number but there was a big church down the street on the corner across from a barbershop and a filling station.

I looked at the street sign where we were and it was West 49th Street which was just on the outskirts of the city all the way across town. I asked him if we had been walking in circles and if the streets ran consecutively, then we were a long way from his sister's house. I suggested that we catch a bus and ride back to 13th Street and he said he didn't have any money.

I only had a bus token myself, so we walked back to the spot where we got off the bus, then Modestine said: "I think we're lost."

"**Lost!**" I think I panicked. I had heard about people getting lost and were never found again and I took it to mean just what it said "**lost.**" It was dark and was getting cold. There weren't many people on the streets. I wanted to cry.

Just as I sat down on a small stone wall and started yelling at Modestine about how stupid this whole thing was, a man with two teenage boys approached us and I asked him if he knew where there was a church on a corner across from a barber shop and a filling station. He said you mean Joe's Barber?

"Yes," I said not knowing whether it was Joe's or Moe's.

"Yeah, that's where I'm going. Gotta take these two heah and git their ears trimmed."

"Can we go with you?" I asked.

"Sho, come on." We walked seven blocks in the opposite direction to East 20th Street and Woodland Avenue and there was the Esso filling station, the barber shop and New Bethel Baptist Church. It was cold so we went into the barber shop to warm up. As we stood by the heater, our guide asked, "Y'all live round heah."

"No suh," Modestine replied.

"Where y'all live?"

"At the orphanage. We're running away," I blurted.

Ooops!

I knew I had goofed the minute I said it. Modestine looked at me as if he could have killed me and I'm sure he would have done just that if he had a weapon.

He said, "We're not running away. I'm just going to live with my sister."

"Who's yo sistuh?"

"Pearl."

"Pearl who?"

"Pearl Counts."

"I know Pearlie Counts. She b'longs ta my church. She got two boys almos' the same age as dese. Dey go to da same school as dese heah. She lives right up the street heah in that big yella house on da lef' hand side o' da street. But I don't blame you boys fuh runnin 'way frum dat place, I wouldn't stey out dere neitha. Tells me dats a mean ole nigga out dere. He beats you kids all da time I heah."

"Yes sir."

When we heard which house she lived in, Modestine and I looked at each other and did an excellent job of not exploding into joy.

We headed for the door and as we were leaving he said, "Tell Pearlie, J.T. said 'hello.'"

"Yes sir."

"We eased the door to the barber shop closed and boy, lookout, we hit the pavement with both feet running after skipping two steps in front of the door. Modestine was trying to keep up with me. I was running as if I were going to **my** sister's house.

We dashed across the lawn, into the enclosed screened porch and into the house. We ran right into the arms of **Mr. Peay**. He was sitting there waiting for us because he knew that we had no place else to go.

He handcuffed us and threw us in the back of the station

wagon he had parked in the alley behind the house. My heartbeat accelerated tremendously. I looked at the cuffs and my thoughts shouted to me—"**Criminal!**"

I had never seen a real pair of handcuffs. I knew that they put them on people who had killed somebody or had done something really bad. I curled into a ball with my face buried in the crevice of the seat and was wishing that I could just die right then and there. Modestine sat in complete silence.

He took us back to the orphanage and beat us terribly. I was tied to a chair with a belt stripped to my waist as he flogged me with the horse strap until all consciousness left me.

When I regained consciousness I was sore from my shoulders to my ankles. My body was completely marked with red welt marks from the blows. I couldn't move so Booster and Henry had to lift me to my bed. I couldn't lie down because of the severe pain. The pain was beyond crying so I stopped. Something happened inside of me and the tears just stopped. Echols and Shoe tried to comfort me and sat and talked with me all night.

During our conversation, I vowed that I would never stay in that place, and just as soon as I was able I would run away again. They begged me not to do it but I was determined to get away from there.

We were both kept from school for two weeks so our wounds could heal and was assigned to do heavy labor each day until late into the night, and at four o'clock the next morning, our feet were out of the bed to begin the next day's chores.

One of our major chores assigned to us while on restriction was to "grub" tree trunks. The tree trunks were oak and maple with diameters spanning three and four feet. Our only tools were a shovel, a mattock, and an axe.

We had to dig a hole and cut the roots almost twice as deep as we were tall until we reached the "tap" root which was the main root of the tree located at the bottom of the stump.

When it rained, it was just another pleasure in our punishment for Peay. For us it was more misery because we worked on the stump whether it rained or not. Sometimes the water filled the hole and we had to bail it out by the bucketfuls and work in mud up to our waists.

After work each day, my back had suffered so much that I could hardly stand straight. Shoe would put hot rags on it for me to help ease the pain.

As I performed these chores, I was constantly thinking to myself of the handcuffs and asking all of the "Why" questions.

The biggest question was: Why am I being treated so mean? I haven't harmed anyone. I have committed no crime. Yet I'm treated as a criminal. My only crime is I don't have any parents and I'm being treated like a dog for just trying to find them.

I prayed often when I was to myself for God to take me away. But the beating I received from Peay put an end to the crying.

Two weeks later, on June 11th, my eleventh birthday, I returned to school and ran away again. This time I went alone. I had no place to go, but I was determined that I would find a job doing something which would give me money for food and I didn't really need to live in a house. I'd sleep outside or just any place that I could.

I had prepared myself for my escape. I told my sister my plans and she kissed me good-bye and said not to worry about her. In my school bag, I had packed all of my school books, some socks and a pair of clean underwear. On my body, I wore two shirts, another pair of pants under my overalls and a sweater. That's all. My sister gave me twenty-five cents to buy bus tokens which were seven cents each.

I caught the city bus from school and rode into the city to a place I felt to be far away from Modestine sister's house. I even transferred from one bus to go across town. My intention was to just get lost. I stopped in a section of the city called Columbia Heights. It was a pretty decent looking area in a black neighborhood.

I went to the community playground to stake out my sleeping quarters and toilet facilities. I played ball with the children until it closed and they left the grounds. I then crawled under the rear of the building where the tools were kept and slept.

This continued for almost three weeks. Each day I read my books and did the homework exercises at the end of each chapter just as if I were still attending school. The groundskeeper caught me as I was crawling from where I "lived." I told him my story and he said he would let me continue to stay so long as I didn't mess with anything.

I silently thanked God and offered to help him with his chores but he declined the offer and told me that I should be in school somewhere. A few days passed and he asked me if I wanted a job washing dishes in a Dairy Queen two nights a week so I could eat.

"Yes sir!"

I got the job and was willing to work for what was given to me to eat plus all I could stuff inside my clothes. The nights when I didn't work, I'd wait until they closed the restaurant and raid the garbage cans for food.

One of the workers at the restaurant was a young white girl who befriended me. She was a very friendly and decent person to me. She would help me with my chores and have long conversations with me which would frighten the daylights out of me because it was in the segregated south when black people were consistently being read about in obituary columns; or in the public record; or not read about; nor heard about; nor seen about either. I didn't want any of this to happen to me.

One Sunday I wanted to go to church and. I put on my best clothes and went and sat on the back pew. The experience was just too much for me to handle. I sat there and in just a matter of minutes, tears began to stream from my eyes.

The minister was reciting the Beatitudes from the fifth chapter of St. Matthew:

Blessed are they which do hunger and thirst after righteousness; for they shall be filled.

Blessed are the peacemakers for they shall be called the children of God.

I didn't know why. I just ran out and was walking down the street when a police car cruised by and stopped. I froze. The policeman got out of the car and walked in my direction. I wanted to flee but I couldn't. I was cemented in my footsteps and just stood there. He looked at me and glanced at a note pad and asked my name. I stammered, "Ugh, Charlie sir, Charlie Broomfield."

He said to me, "I know it son. We have been looking for you. I've seen you a few times before at the playground, but I didn't pick you up because you were not a bad boy. But I need to take you back before something bad happens to you.

I want you to go back and get it straightened out there. You can't spend the rest of your life running and hiding. We've been getting some reports from people about how bad it is out there."

When he said that to me, all of the fright left me. I didn't fear Peay anymore. I was determined that he would not whip me again as he did before.

Remember the rake? Peay does.

Twelve

Be Fruitful . . .

I looked at the clock on the table next to my bed which read eight o'clock. I snapped out of my thoughts and sprang from the bed admonishing myself for sleeping so late.

Gosh, I would be late for Andrew. I hope he doesn't think I'm not coming. I dashed through the door just as I heard my mother yell, "Don't you stay up dere too long, I wonts you ta come back heah and hep me straighten out dis heah house." Her words fell in a heap on the floor.

I dashed up the hill and there sat Andrew sitting on the lawn talking with Pohaku. Andrew asked me if it would be alright if Pohaku joined us in the discussion."

"Pohaku? Wow, how neat! Yes he can because I have all kinds of questions to ask him."

I had been thinking about Pohaku since Andrew told me about the acorns and I wanted to ask him just how many acorns were there. We walked in the direction of Andrew's room and as we were walking, Andrew turned to me and asked, "Amos, why do you think that your father named you after him? Why did he wait until you were born to give you his name? And you, of all of the rest of the brothers, knows him the least."

"I don't know. What do you think?"

Pohaku chimed in: "How many sons are there?"

"It would have been eight counting Charlie. I'm number seven."

He then asked: "How many children all together?"

I counted: "It would have been twelve?"

His eyes widened as he whirled in front of me and looked into my face and exclaimed: "You are the seventh son, and the eleventh child."

"So?" I asked. "What does that mean?"

Pohaku stated, "It means that you are extraordinarily gifted. But you will suffer greatly from these very gifts that you possess. You have a very strong spiritual base and will become a social prick to small minded individuals and things that you feel are unjust. You will constantly be in search of something—but seldom finding it. You are going to have to travel far and wide in search of it. But once it is found you will reap great rewards."

"Hunh? Searching for what? I don't understand what you mean?"

He looked at Andrew then to me, his eyes were widened and glazed and said, "You will be constantly reaching and pulling and people around you are going to dispel you completely or totally become enraptured with you. You are going to make tremendous impressions upon people—one way or the other and you will not seek glorification for your acclaims. By your unassuming demeanor, people will mistake your strengths for weaknesses and seek to take undue advantage of you but they will do so at their peril."

By then, we had reached the room and I was befuddled and totally confused about what he said. I was still intrigued with the acorns, nonetheless.

Andrew looked at the puzzled look on my face and said: "You'll find out the meaning to what Pohaku was saying to you. But count on it—every word he has spoken is true. And you should also think about why daddy gave you his name and why you and Helen don't get along with each other. But I'll just tell you this much about the name "Amos." It is indeed a very strong name befitting a very strong individual.

Amos was a prophet who lived in Samaria about 750 B.C. He had the gift of prophecy, meaning he could tell you about the future before it happened. He was a rude, powerfully built man with strong legs, harsh speech and lived a rather simple life.

He was the first prophet to set down his message about justice in writing. He fiercely denounced the wrong doing of the king, the noblemen, and especially the priests. He protested against empty and meaningless forms of religion, and detested ignorance.

He was not against organized religion, but he insisted that men should not serve God only through sacrifice and prayer, but by justice and mercy to his neighbor. He preached the doctrine of righteousness with tremendous force and was highly indignant at the mean treatment of the poor people in Israel.

He preached that his God was a God of Justice, and told Israel to 'let your judgement run down as waters, and righteousness as a mighty stream before the wrath of God is visited upon you.'

Be Fruitful...

Also, the number seven is a holy number. I'll give you just a few quips and superstitions surrounding this number. There were seven days in creation; seven days in a week; seven divisions in the Lord's Prayer; seven phases of the moon; seven phases of life; seven Bibles; seven deadly sins; seven virtues; seven spirits of God; seven wonders of the world; and the highest level of heaven is the Seventh Heaven.

I know what's going on between you and Helen. You two will never be able to get along. But I know that you will find it out for yourself. Once you make this discovery, then you will be ready to leave—but now is not the time.

I'm sure she had something to say to you this morning before you came up to visit. I also know that when you get home today, it would do you well to leave everything just as they are and put off any plans of leaving until later on.

I listened to him intently and was guided by all of his advice which served me well in later years. We began our discussion about the forbidden fruit and what it represented.

Pohaku and I sat on the floor. Andrew sat in his chair at his desk and began:

> It bothers me to great length to see that the theologians used allegory and figure of speech to instill upon us by way of eating a piece of fruit some ethical standard.
>
> By the simple act of a physical function we come into a system of human relationships since some pious editor took the liberty to call Eve Adam's wife. God

didn't. Genesis tells us that He said He would give him a help mate. Not a wife.

And so we now have the necessary standards of what is required to have children—a wife and a husband—a family; not a man and a help mate; not two divine individuals created in Divine imagery who were void of all prurient interests that have been ascribed with the sexual act.

Let's look at this thing called family. It is a very relevant topic now for you, Amos and I want you to understand it if not from an historical perspective.

He paused.

I want to say to you before we start, that there is a lack of ability, preparation, and time on my part to enter into a limitless debate on this subject. Perhaps this is something you might want to pursue further. Okay?

But, as you recall, the Adam and Eve family began in or about 850 B.C. at the earliest. Well, let me take you back a few centuries earlier.

The first historical actions to inaugurate any set of rules or ethics for man and woman in their sexual relation was Menes, first King of Egypt about 3,500 years B.C.

Prior to this, there is no other historical account except those given in the Old Testament when men **took** to themselves wives and concubines according to their own desires and without any restraint.

And even so, it is either by sloppy omission of the writers of the story of Adam and Eve, or a clear yet vexatious admission of the ruling class that allowed them unbridled access to engage in sexual intercourse with women of the lower cast.

Recall chapter six verses 1-2: 'that the sons of God saw the daughters of men that they were fair: and they took them wives of all which they chose.' If they were the sons of God what restrictions were placed upon them as to how many wives to have or in what manner they should conduct their sexual activities.

It is up to you whether you buy the belief that the entire human family came from one pair. But history, both sacred and profane, point to polygamy as the oldest form of marriage.

Now if Adam had only one wife, it was due to circumstances beyond his control. There were no other women around. What might have prevented him from having more wives than Eve if there were other women?

And if you follow the flow of history and the current of social institutions, you will find that they don't change that rapidly.

Pay close attention to my next comments. Not too far down the family history in Adam's genealogical tree, we find his descendent Lamech with two wives.

Again, in Noah's time the sons of God were freely having intercourse and taking wives. The world became so wicked that God had to send a big wash and wipe the slate clean and start all over again.

Yet it didn't remain clean. Old Abraham, Father of the Hebrews when he went down to Egypt to avoid the famine was faced with a life and death situation because the Pharaoh saw his wife Sara and she was fair and he desired her.

What did Abraham do? To save his own neck, he said to Pharaoh, she is my sister, not my wife and Pharaoh took her as his wife until funny things started to happen to him—we don't know what they were since no medical records were maintained then, but he sent Sara back to Abraham.

Additionally, recall the sixteenth chapter of Genesis: "Now Sara, Abraham's wife bare him no children; and she had a hand-maid, an **Egyptian**, whose name was Hagar.

And Sara said unto Abraham, 'Behold now, the Lord hath restrained me from bearing children; I pray thee, **go in unto my maid**; it may be that I may obtain children by her. And he went in unto Hagar, and she conceived.'

Wow! Some pretty heavy stuff I said to myself. But I needed to be more specific in my understanding of all of this, so I asked: Isn't Egypt located in Africa? Was Hagar an African woman living in a place called Egypt? If Abraham had a son by her, did this mean that he had an "illegitimate" African-Egyptian son? What happened to him? I have only heard that Abraham had the "Big Two," Isaac and Jacob. This was supposed to be the beginning of the nation of Israel wasn't it?

Andrew looked at me with a gleeful smirk as he uttered:

You think you're so smart. Well let me tell you something, you have just hit upon one of the world's best kept secrets. You should look into this as your mind continues to become infatuated with seeking the truth. But let me continue our present discussion. Okay?

Abraham wasn't finished yet. He had another wife named Keturah and had six sons by her. I'm not positive if Sara was still on the scene or not, but the Hagar tryst certainly gives us our first case of adultery, or if not, then we had a marriage system which was either polygamous or concubinage.

And then we find Moses about 16 B.C. who laid down a variety of rules and regulations regarding intercourse between man and woman.

Then look at King David, 'the man after God's own heart,' who disobeyed the Mosaic laws by having concubines and committing adultery with Bath-sheba, the wife of Uriah, who was sent on a suicide mission which caused his death so David could marry her. She became the mother of Solomon who imprisoned ten of his seven hundred wives because they were having sex with his son Absolom.

The next historical efforts to regulate sexual relations were instituted in China by Emperor Fu-hi in 2,650 B.C.

Cecrops, in 1550 B.C. concocted a code for the Greeks but they were social in nature—not legal. Additional accounts which I'm sure you can relate to, will show that when men were at war with each other, the victors carried off the captured treasures and women to their kings and they distributed the bounty amongst the kings and soldiers.

The treasure was called the **bounty** which was carried in a boot—suitcase, truck, vault or whatever. The name "booty" was eventually applied to all of the captured treasures which included the women.

This is where we get the expression; 'getting some booty' came from.

I cleared my throat and looked out the window and began to reminisce.

Oh yeah, my mind did a quick flashback to when I was in the Baby Cottage. I remember we used to say "booty" all of the time in the orphanage. Cornrows said it when we were in the Baby Cottage quite a lot.

He would disappear sometimes and I'd ask him where he had been and he would say, "getting some booty." I asked him where did he go to get the booty. He wouldn't say. Booty must have been very hard to get because I never saw him bring back anything in his pockets or in his hands.

However, he used to go get it all the time. I asked when he got it what did he do with it. Was it good? Could you eat it? I also asked if I could go with him the next time he went to get some. He said, "No, one day you'll find out, but you can only get it from the girls." Only the girls had the booty. I had a sneaking suspicion as to what it was.

He got his booty all the time from Juanita and my sister. I used to see May and Henry together many times before he went out to get his booty. Modestine used to get his booty from Fannie May; Eldrine got his from Hattie, but sometimes he got his from Mary; Lonnie got his from Annie and Mary; Booster got his from Estelle and also from Mary; Joe Lewis with his teeny weeny got his from Teresa, who had to show him how to get it; Snipper could only get his from Ula Mae (Fatso, a big, black, greasy girl who was crazy about Snipper), but he really wanted Deloris. Mr. Peay got his from Miss Pounds and any of the other "big girls" he wanted.

He mainly got it from Deloris, his little red-bone pet who ruled the roost in the Girls Dormitory.

It seemed as if all of the older boys got booty, and so I asked Leyla did she have any booty, and if she did, would she give me some. She slapped my face.

I later found out what booty was when Cornrows and Juanita were caught in the dirty linen closet getting booty. Miss Pounds had gone to the linen closet to put in some of Deedy's wet sheets. When she opened the door, she saw a bundle of dirty clothes move and she yanked back the bundle and there lay Cornrows and Juanita.

She beat the living stuffing out of both of them. My sister told me they were caught "doing something nasty" and that it was a nasty thing to do, so I stayed away from it—at least until I was nine years old; then I cussed her out. Leyla gave me some booty. Hmnnn!

Andrew's voice again pierced my treasured thoughts as he seemed to have noticed that I had drifted off into some other space.

"You see, it goes on and on, but as I said, I don't have time, even in this place to carry it any further."

I thought it was very interesting and I was still revved up with the expectations that Pohaku would speak. He said nothing. He just sat there in deep thought.

There was a very pregnant pause in the room when Pohaku barked:

> All of this damn talk about sex has gotten this whole world hung up about nothing. So much so, that these whitewashed Christians have come up with some God Almighty stupid stuff.

First they came up with this original sin crap, then a virgin birth, and worst of all, immaculate conception.

Listen to this crap. First, they concocted a premise that we are sinful, even before we take our first breath on this earth because our parents were sinful.

Now tell me this—if I'm sinful by virtue of my birth to a legitimate set of parents, then how much more sinful are the infants that are not born with the same stamp as myself.

I sat there glued to every word he said but it was getting to be a little confusing to me so I asked him what he meant. He explained:

I'm talking about a child born out of wedlock, children born with handicaps, children born as a result of the mother being a victim of rape. And what about children born with a different skin color than mine. Were their births more sinful than mine?

So what did these idiots do since they boxed us all in a corner and painted us all as **sinful?** They had to stretch this autonomic thinking process which we were all born into with their concocted supplanted thinking morass in order to provide us with another notion called redemption. Redemption from what—from being born? How, might I ask, and by what mechanism? Death? **Bull Corn!**

Since sexual commerce was so distasteful to them, they had to concoct a vehicle to provide for a redeemer which can only come from God. Recall the Adam story when God made the beasts from the dust and He wanted Adam to be able to communicate with the animals, so He had to make Adam out of the dust also, because the other inhabitants in the Garden were angels whom even Adam could not communicate with.

So this redeemer must also be 'bones of our bones and flesh of our flesh' and readily assessable to and understood by the human brain—of necessity it had to be in human form.

Now, since we have swallowed the "man" line from Adam as first man and to his Creator as "Him," the redeemer was also to be a man—we were given a boy; baby Jesus.

But man had to be born to woman because the days of miracles had run out and the birth of a **Man-God** could not be directly involved in this humanly sinful sexual act.

So the Man-God had to issue from a **married virgin** who had defied the natural laws of her marriage by not having sexual intercourse with her husband thereby stretching this supplanted thought to even more ridiculous extremes. This is tantamount to saying 'this blue shirt is yellow.'

"Wait a minute, are you saying that Mary and Joseph were married to each other and didn't have sex until after Jesus was born? I wonder how Joseph felt when he found out that his wife was pregnant and he hadn't had sex with her. If I were him, I'd be really mad at her."

Pohaku continued:

Well, that's the way the story is told but let me finish and you can draw your own conclusions about the efficacy of all this. But for now, let's look at the miracle of incarnation which means that a human can embody the divine qualities of a divine being.

I ask you, if, in the first place, you can believe in the Divine Being as being omnipotent that is, all-power, then these divine qualities can be just as easily given to a child born under "normal" conditions as well as a child born under "special" conditions.

If your faith is strong enough to accept and believe one such miracle, then any other divine miracle would work just as well.

Immaculate conception could very well be called immaculate deception as well as all the other supplanted thought given to us as truth.

In this case, **two** miracles had to happen. First, the taint of the original sin on the side of the father, Joseph, had to be removed, so Joseph's sperm had to be substituted with a holy solution, with life-giving qualities and human characteristics. Second, the mother could not be avoided. The baby had to come from her womb, **but** it had to be a sinless womb, can you imagine that. Some wombs are sinful; some wombs are more sinful than others. It seems to me that if a woman has not given birth to a child, then her womb is less sinful than one who has. Unless of course there are no degrees of sinful wombs.

If this is not the case, why wasn't a woman with a less sinful womb chosen for the job and make the job easier. Why not get a true virgin instead of recycling one?

Was Mary's womb sinful before she bore Jesus and it became sinless when she had Him and would revert back to being sinful when giving birth after Jesus?

Poppycock of the first order!

Thirteen

To Dust Thou Shall Return . . .

I looked at my watch; it was three o'clock and we had talked through lunch. I said to Andrew that I must go home and help my mother clean. He reminded me to keep calm and don't do anything that I would regret later on. I thanked him and Pohaku and walked home.

As I walked into the house she told me to sweep and mop the whole house which included the living room, kitchen, her bedroom, May and Linda's room, my room, the bathroom, Thomas and Peter's room, and Butch's room. I did all of the chores without saying a word. When I finished she told me to rake the yard and empty the rubbish from the many overflowing barrels into the large dumpster, and to sweep off the back porch.

When I finished she called me into her room and said, "Charlie, I don't want you to be going up dere to dat hospital no mo, and be wit Andrew. Roseanne don' told me 'bout some of da stupid stuff you been talkin 'bout. I don't wont you comin' in dis house talkin' bout all dat ole junk 'bout Jesus."

"My name is not Charlie. My name is Amos."

"What you say boy?"

"My name is not Charlie. My real name is Amos."

"Lord, now who don went 'n put dat stuf' in yo head? Did you ben talkin' wid yo daddy."

"Andrew told me that my real name is Amos, just like my daddy's name is Amos. And I don't want you to call me 'Charlie' anymore."

"Now I knows you betta stey way frum dere. Yo name is Charlie. I'm yo mama and I oughtta know what I named my chilluns."

"What about the baby that was dead when he was born? Wasn't his name Charlie?"

"Andrew tol' you dat?"

"Yes he did, and you have been calling me Charlie thinking that I was that dead baby all these years. I'm gonna find out what my real name is and what my daddy's name is."

"I don' tol you dat yo name is Charlie. Now git outta heah."

Listening to Andrew's advice not to mess up, I bit my tongue and left the house. While I was sitting on the bannister outside the front entrance, my sister Linda popped up and said, "My goodness, what in the world is bothering you? You look like the whole world is going to come to an end."

"Linda," I asked, "is my name Charlie or Amos?"

"As far as I know your name is Charlie. That's all I've ever known you by. Where did you get this 'Amos' from?"

"Is daddy's name 'Amos' or Willie."

"His name is William. But, I've heard some people call him Amos. Aunt Ruth calls him Amos sometimes. Why don't you ask her. She'll tell you. Anything I want to know about the family, I go to her and Uncle Randy. She's daddy's sister and she's the only one in this whole family who I think has any kind of sense.

"You should also talk to cousin Rene or even Ronald. You ain't gonna get anything out of these Broomfields. They don't care about anybody but themselves. Especially that mother of ours. You'll see for yourself if you haven't already."

When she said this, my brows furrowed and my eyes popped out. I didn't know she felt that way about our mother. I do know that she was very seldom at home. She spent most of her time with daddy and aunt Ruth. I was relieved to find out that I wasn't alone in feeling about my mother as I did. I suspected Andrew had his feelings, but he had risen above showing any emotions about her.

I began to spend a lot of time with my cousin Ronald, Uncle Randy, and Aunt Ruth, specially Uncle Randy and Ronald. To me, other than my brothers Andrew, James, Peter, and my sister Linda, they were my family.

Uncle Randy was a grand old man. He and his brother Uncle Jimmy were from the Islands. They both had a fresh open face coated with smooth ebony skin and dazzling bleached ivory teeth carved to perfection.

He had an intensely soft smile which he could hold indefinitely. When they both laughed, the whole area lit up; not from the glow from their teeth, but from the jubilance in the atmosphere.

He enjoyed teasing me about being so naive and uninformed. But he never tried to embarrass me. He would watch me try to do something which he felt any boy my age should have knowledge of and laugh his head off when I goofed and say his famous saying, "Boy, don't you know anything at all."

He felt that every boy should know how to fix a car and to drive it.

Uncle Randy owned several multi-unit apartment buildings and Cousin Ronald and I were paid to clean the furnaces, haul away the rubbish, and collect the rent for him. This was a fun thing for us. Ronald taught me how to drive the beat up dump truck and we would go speeding throughout the city collecting rent and having a good time spending some of it. It didn't matter to Uncle Randy how much we spent, he would just take it out of our pay checks.

Ronald had privileges to drive their shiny new Cadillac car on weekends and we'd ride around Worcester picking up girls. We were not allowed to cruise on the side of the city I lived. We always had to stay on his side of town.

They lived in the east side of the city in a very nice neighborhood. The college was nearby. There were single family homes with well-kept lawns in an integrated neighborhood. I liked to go there and stay days at a time. Ronald was viewed as being "stuck-up" and snobbish by other members of the family, especially my mother. They would rag me for "hanging around him," saying I was trying to be like him.

Aunt Ruth was just like the mother I had envisioned for myself. She and daddy looked almost like twins. Her Native American features were more pronounced than his because she wore her hair in long pony tails around the house, and wore many Native American artifacts made of sterling silver and topaz.

She and I had long hours of discussions about everything. Our discussions were mainly concerned with growing up and future expectations for what we wanted out of life. I never had any one who seemed to be concerned with my future as she and Uncle Randy. They both stressed the importance of going to good schools and to learn how to get along with other people outside of my immediate range of association.

After a while, Andrew did not come home often anymore because of his health. He told me during one of my visits during the early part of September that he didn't feel as if I would be seeing him much longer because he had developed cancer. It was in its terminal stages and the authorities have decided that an operation would not be beneficial.

I visited him almost everyday after that. During one of my visits, Pohaku came and brought us tea and we chatted. As we sat there, I began to feel that Andrew was telling me "goodbye" as he said that he wanted me to continue to come and visit Pohaku. I said that I would and I also wanted to continue to study and learn all I could about the things we had discussed.

He said, "You've got the best teacher sitting beside you. He taught me all that I know." I didn't feel too saddened by his impending death. He had prepared me for this. We had discussed previously about endings—which were only another beginning.

He had said to me on a previous occasion that contrary to popular belief, in the beginning was the end. He had told me that when God, through His creation, gave us intelligence, He ended ignorance. We took this intelligence and began to produce all of the things around us to make our lives work for us.

With these thoughts drumming through my head I stopped by the house on my way to Ronald's and my mother was sitting in the living room with Roseanne and two other people discussing the Bible. She yelled, "Come in heah Charlie, you needs ta heah som' o' dis."

"Yeah, he surely does," said Roseanne.

I sat down and heard some of the most ridiculous crap ever. The discussion was about Jesus and servants and how 144,000 angels will go out and teach people and people would be coming out of their graves and Jesus would be sitting next to God and sending people to be fried and how the world would be destroyed and I would be one of the first ones fried if I didn't straighten up.

There were all sorts of pamphlets spread out on the table. One, in particular caught my eye, it was entitled *Awake*. I looked at it and said to myself, I certainly wished these people would do just that.

The discussion about Jesus continued and Roseanne turned to me and asked me in a very condescending way, "Do you know about Jesus? Have you ever heard of Him? Do you know who He was?"

I couldn't hold back any longer, "Yes, I know. Do you? Does any one of you know about Him and who He was? I'll tell you since you asked me. He was a boy born to the parents, Mary and Joseph who grew up and became a preacher."

"Now you see, I knew you didn't know who he was. You think you're so smart. He was not a preacher. He was Jesus Christ, God on earth," she said.

I leaned forward and looked her straight in the eye and said, "He was no more God than you or I or any one else in this room. He was an example of what we all have in us and what we can become."

"Now you shet yo mouth boy or I'll make an example outta you. I don' wanna heah you say Jesus was not God," my mother blurted.

I looked at her and said, "Jesus was the name that was given to the boy just like the name 'Charlie' or 'Amos' or whoever, was given to me. The word 'Christ is just a title given to Him, the same as Mr. or Mrs., or doctor, or lawyer, or president, or preacher, or anything else. It means Messiah, or Messenger, or Savior, or Redeemer, or Salvation, or anything else you might want to loosely call it."

"Shet up boy, I don tol yo 'bout talking dat ol stuff, fo I slap yo face," said my mother.

"You do so and you'll regret it too." The words snapped out of my mouth without me really knowing that I had said it.

"No, let him go on. Continue with what you were saying. It sounds really interesting," said one of the ladies.

I was emboldened now so I said to them, "There was no more God in Jesus than there is in any one of you or I. There was more **Christ** in Him than you or I because He was a total messenger. His entire life was devoted to speaking of loving one another, peace, abundance, goodness, and truth. This is what a savior or a messiah or what have you, is all about. Now how many of you have a life that is totally dedicated to just one of the things that I mentioned about the Christ in Jesus? Not one of you. You speak about God. You say that Jesus was God who came down on earth to save us. How many of you know what God is?"

"God is in charge of all of heaven who will come down here and save all of the people who listen to His word. And you better start to listen, too," blurted Roseanne.

I became more irritated with her. I asked her, "Why are you referring to God as 'Him?'"

"Because He is. He ain't no woman. He is a spirit."

Wow! I thought to myself. What a small mind. Look at

the damage that has been done to both my mother and my sister. I tried to keep an open mind and went back into the discussion.

"Then," I asked, "can a spirit be a person?"

"God is not a person. God is just **It**," said one of the ladies.

"Well, if God is just **It**, then how can we as humans make any descriptive attributes to a spirit or an **It**? Has anyone in this room ever seen a spirit? I don't think so. To me, God is Being. Just as she pointed out. God is neither good nor bad. God just is. Once we begin to say that God is good, we then begin to put our own attributes and projections of what we think of as good or bad. What is Good today may be Bad tomorrow. What is good to us in this room may not be good to the people across the street selling dope.

(I had to pause when I said that, because I silently realized, what's the difference, this poison or that poison).

"When we say that God is all power, knows everything, and is everywhere, then let me ask you this. If God is everything, is there anything **more than everything**? That's what the word means—**every thing;** all things; nothing else; nothing more. This is opposed to the words **nothing**, which means **no thing**, or **something** which means **some thing**."

"But God does not represent evil. The devil represent evil," shouted Roseanne.

"Are you saying that evil is something outside of good or God? Something else other than everything. If you are, then you are saying that God does not have **all** of the power; God is **not** everything or **all** things."

"Yeah, Satan represents the power of evil. God only represents good."

"Didn't I just tell you that God is all power. There is no such thing as God and. . . or God plus. . . There is nothing beyond everything."

I was getting a little bit worked up, so I took a deep breath and looked away from her. My eyes fell upon the lady sitting across from me who seemed to be staring at me all of the time. Our eyes met briefly and she immediately dropped her glance to the coffee table in front of us.

"Well, you're wrong. God does not represent evil. The devil represents evil. Not God. And this is what I believe in and you're not gonna change it," shouted Roseanne.

"Roseanne," I said, "I'm not trying to change anything that you or anybody else believe. But I'm just trying to get you to see for yourself. Now let me ask you this very simple question:

'If you had all of the money, all of the power, all the love, all goodness, and every possession that you wanted; if you had all of these things and had God as the foundation of your belief, would you have any more than if you had only God?'

"I don't understand what you're talking about. God doesn't have anything to do with this world. God is in charge of heaven not this world. Satan has taken over this world. God will take all of His people to heaven and destroy this world. That's why He had to come down here as a man and sacrifice Himself on the cross so His people would be saved."

She turned and looked at my mother who was sitting back in her chair with her arms folded and her eyes rolling around in her head as she nodded it slightly when Roseanne spoke, "Mama, this boy is crazy. How can you put up with him? I don't even want to be around him anymore. All he has been doing is sitting here talking about blasphemy. You know you raised us better than that."

"Unh Hunh. Sounds jes lak his father. His father used ta say som' o' dose very same things."

I looked at both of them with distant eyes and said to myself: "Who are these people? Are they both relics from an ancient wreck? Where does sanguinity ends and ignorance begins?" My eyes danced back and forth between them and silently commended them both for their small-minded persistence. It was beautiful, just as the persistence of cancer is beautiful.

The lady who was sitting across from me hurriedly began to gather the magazines from the table and putting them into her pouch while gazing at me without saying a word. Some of the papers became rumpled, but she didn't straighten them out. She just shoved them deeper into the pouch.

Her companion stood and said, "Helen we got to be going, and I'll call you and come by to see you when we can sit down without being interrupted."

As she spoke, her eyes darted spears of steel at me as she was leaving. Her companion twitched a little soft smile at me as she stood, and I stole it.

At my early age, I could discern that she had an Evesque frame beneath her formless grey dress, but my cupidity was curbed by the limitation of my "innocent" youth.

I got up to leave the room and my mother said to me, "Frum here on out, I don't wont you ta go back up ta dat hospita no 'mo."

"Try and stop me," I snapped.

"You heard what your mother said. And I want you to stay away from my house with that old mess," snapped Roseanne.

"You don't have to worry about me ever coming to your house. And besides, I'm leaving this place. If any one of you in this messed up family ever see me again, it would be too soon."

I left and went to my room, picked up a few things, and went to Aunt Ruth's house. I stayed there for about a month and I continued to make short visits to see Andrew everyday.

I could see him leaving us with each visit. He finally became too weak to walk and would not eat much of anything. During my visits, I would just sit at his bedside in silence and hold his hands in mine as well as both of our thoughts. Every breath was laborious for him and I wished I could breathe for him.

On one of my visits, I told him about the conversation with Roseanne and my mother. He looked at me, touched by shoulder, and said in a very authoritative voice:

> Now you are free to leave anytime you wish, but Pohaku has a few things he wants to tell you before you leave. Will you promise me to stay at least until you've heard what he has to say? And then you can go about your father's business.

"What do you mean my father's business?"
He said:

> It simply means to learn to develop your own thought potential; to preserve your right to think for yourself; and to live in the presence of God's holy wisdom because this wisdom is divine and is all based upon loving one another. It is that simple. It is not to be theorized and debated, but it should be lived. Also, promise me that you will never debate God's wisdom with

anyone. Nor will you be judgmental in dealing with other people. The world is innately just and it will withstand its course without you judging it. Also, never let anyone else decide for you what is right or wrong. If the idea is good and is based upon your faith in the truthfulness of it, then go ahead with it.

I want you to learn how to be patient with others. From my observation of you, you are a very impatient person. But take time to listen to what others have to say and respect their views. And I implore you not to try to impress your views on to theirs.

Another thing to remember—don't get caught up in this spiritual arrogance which is now sweeping the world. Christians carry no more weight in the sight of God than do the Buddhists, or the Zionists or the Moslems. They are all the same to the Creator. Jesus never heard of a Christian and to that end, I have never seen one either. A Christian is a person who would want the very same "good" for his neighbor as he would want for himself. They are Christians when they can love their enemies and their neighbors as they love themselves. Seen any of those lately? I haven't. Just do your spiritual work and you will be blessed.

Have faith in yourself and in others because God has allotted tasks for all of us. You've got a big task ahead of you just as your father had. He did the best he could with what he had. Being a junkman and losing his arm was not a pleasant thing for him. Having all these children and his relationship with Helen was also not pleasant either. Ask your sister Linda about him, she knows him better than the other children.

Sometimes it will be a bit burdensome and your tasks may not be what you seemingly want to do. But perform them with love, dignity, and grace. This should always be your first and last concern. Okay?

"Unh Hunh."

As you can see, there is a dearth of love and support in this family as in most families, but keep at it and you will find that there is a lot of wisdom here which needs to be tapped into and channeled in the right direction.

This family is just like seeds cast into the wind. Some of the seeds will fall on shallow soil and grow quickly into beautiful flowers, but also will just as quickly wither and fade away.

Others will fall on a rock or some hard soil and be blown away with the wind and never be seen or heard of. While some will fall onto fertile soil and their roots will become firmly enriched with the soil, and they will grow into firm and beautiful flowers which will withstand the wind and the storm. Do you understand what I'm saying?

"Yes I do."

He reached into his desk drawer and took out a little velvet pouch and handed it to me. "Here, I want you to have this. Keep it with you at all times."

I thanked him and promised him that I would and asked him if I could see it now or later.

"Go ahead and look. This is something I have had for a very long time, and now I want you to have it."

I opened the pouch and there was a beautiful medallion made of pure silver encased with an edging of granite stone. It was painted with a blue background with an "X" insignia painted in white.

I marvelled at it as if it was something sacred. I asked him what it meant and he said it was the sign of the "fallen cross."

He said that the Christians have taken the message out of the teachings of Jesus and replaced it with symbols.

"Take a look at this "symbol" to remind you how meaningless and vexatious those symbols of Christian atheism are to you when you see them. I want you to go and read chapter 2:17 in the Book of Revelations. Okay?"

I hugged him and placed the tightly-held gift in my pocket and sat. As I sat there I couldn't hold back the cascade of tears as they flooded my face with a deep dank sadness.

Andrew then said:

Oh, by the way, I want you to stop worrying so much. You will worry yourself to death if you don't. Let me just tell you this: If you can help a thing to happen or can do something about a certain thing, do not worry, but go to work and help it. If you cannot, do not worry about it, but wait and reserve your strength until you can do something.

You know, I have seen some people during their life have a great many troubles, most of which never happened. I want you to do all you can calmly and plan well and wisely as you can and hope for the best, and take the worst when it really comes. I want you to stop worrying and pick up your load and carry it bravely while over-stepping the burdens in your path, and don't be cheated out of the best that life has to offer. Okay?

I decided long ago that since I have got to die but just once, instead of making it my life-long work, I am going to live while I do live and in the best sense I know how, then die all at once and be done with it. It was not worthwhile for me to die piece-meal by spreading it over years and making my life and others filled with misery and darkness.

I want you to understand that life is not a barter. We are sadly mistaken when we think that spiritual good can be gained by self-denial. We have been told that *I came to give you life. . .abundantly" so learn to eat, drink, and be merry with the fruits of love and goodness of today, and know that you shall not die tomorrow. Today's wedding feast is open only to those who are equipped to enjoy its festivities.*

Cut through the old supplanted thought that if you deny this world another world is secured as a reward. Discard this aversion to the world we live in and learn what it is to truly enjoy the love and goodness of the present. You don't have to go looking through a telescope to find something that is already closer to you than breath.

For myself, I certainly don't want to wait until I die before I can begin to live, and you shouldn't either. These atheists running through our lives masquerading themselves as Christians have dwelled too long on the idea that we must postpone our highest good to an uncertain future. We have been taught that life on this earth is just a "holding pattern" and so we have been living in just a dream of "heaven."

Rather than reconstruct the world in which we find

ourselves, we have been sleepwalking and willing to postpone our good things for another unknown which we have pictured as waiting for us to come and take up our habitat which is already peopled with congenial spiritual celebrities who are enjoying their rewards.

I must say to you that the religion which feeds itself on the emotions of the life that is to come rather than one which applies itself to the duties of the hour is worthless. It is nothing more than mere hypnotism.

I would venture to say to you that I believe that heaven is doubtless a very great disappointment to most of its inhabitants, and I feel strongly that this is no fanciful speculation, but if it is, then present to me the debaters who can convince me otherwise.

Remember, this world is **our** problem. If we focus on it with all our spiritual powers, we will discover that it is not the "desert" upon which cursed is the ground on which we walk; rather, it is sacred and hallowed ground. It is a Garden of delights, a veritable Eden to those who are not blind and can see behind the folly of the fig leaf. What right or reason do we have to suppose a "Paradise Lost" or even to anticipate a "Paradise Regained?"

If you will stay and listen, Pohaku will tell you in more detail than I have time for, that God cannot do any more for you in the future than that which He is doing for you right now. There is no problem which belongs to you right now which cannot be solved.

You will also learn later on in life whether you go to college or not, that true sociology, like botany, is a science of root culture. And, as you mature in your thinking as an artist, you will find that it is not possible to paint the leaves of a tree and enjoy the taste of its fruits and show an appreciation of its loveliness and how wonderfully it relates to its environment unless you understand the workings of the sap which comes from it roots.

Finally, as I pointed out to you earlier, you will also come to know that you have all of the factors of an earthly paradise within yourself. That temple "within you" can never be built by any human hands but your own. So learn to mix the mortar and cut the timbers and plant the seeds of growth with confidence in the crucible of truth as you know it, then you will find that the Tree of Life standing in the midst of your Garden, like the mango tree of the tropics, or the banana tree of the forest, or the richly laden vines of the valley, will all bear in the same season as yours, bud, blossom, and fruit—then you will know that God gave to you *richly all things to enjoy.* Okay?"

"Okay," I repeated. "Wow! And I will stay and listen to Pohaku. I'm much stronger now about how I feel about myself and I don't care what other people may think about me either," I choked.

"Good," he said, "now get out of here and let me get some rest."

This was the last time I saw him alive.

I sauntered home in a deep mist and turned to Revelations 2:17. My jaws dropped as I read: *He that have an ear, let him hear... To him that overcomes will I give to eat of the hidden manna, and will give him a white stone, and in the stone a new name written, which no man knows except he that receives it.*

Wow. Is Andrew some sort of Spirit? How could he know all of these things? He was supposed to be some sort of "nut." I tried to figure what it all meant.

One Thursday morning, on the 30th of November, around ten o'clock, a messenger sent me a feeling that Andrew was dead.

Just a little past noon, I was in the backyard talking to Aunt Ruth when the phone rang. It was the hospital giving us the news that Andrew was dead. He had passed at two minutes past ten. They wanted to know if we could come and claim his belongings since my mother had told them that she didn't have a way to get there.

Aunt Ruth and I went to the hospital where Pohaku was standing beside his bed in a reverential bow with his hands clasped together. He was dressed in a white floor length gown and appeared to be some place else, beyond this room. His face was dressed with authority, as if he were conducting spiritual business in another space. He spoke a few words which were inaudible and invisible to me. My spiritual ears heard him say, "It is finished."

Aunt Ruth and I paused for a moment and did not disturb him. He touched Andrew's forehead with his finger and murmured a few more inaudible words before looking away with an expression which carried finality.

I approached the bed holding onto Aunt Ruth's hand. My eyes were glued to his frail body lying beneath the sheets. There were no tears. The room was lit very brightly although the skies were overcast outside. This seemed to be a new kind of light which was filled with energy and electricity. I had to squint my eyes because of the brightness.

Aunt Ruth stood in silence like a strong oak tree as she focused on Pohaku. As I stood looking down into Andrew's face, my mind ejected all other thoughts except the ones I always felt with him. These were thoughts of innocence and purity; of seeking and finding; of teaching and learning; of loving and wanting to be loved, all of which were deeply delightful to me.

At one time, I felt that Andrew and all of the dwellers in the hospital were just as childlike as myself. And, as I looked at his surroundings where he spent more than half of his life, while the other half was spent in the embrace of a family with no arms, I too wanted to ask the question, "Can any good thing come from Nazareth?"

As I stood there in my thoughts, the melody of my questions joined in with the lyrics of his answers and then became the sweet music of a childish voice enraptured in holy harmlessness and with heavenly grace. I listened and it felt good.

Andrew had shed new light upon the sacred word of God for me. He had unlocked the key and cracked the door to finding the answers to the secrets of each of the seven brief ages which a man passes throughout this life, i.e.; infancy, boyhood, adolescence, youth, the prime, the fall, and the winter.

For him, he had already found his Parent-God. His human spirit knew the truth and the mystery of mysteries which no one but himself could fully understand. He knew that in him, God was made manifest in flesh and he carried this with him as his guide on this earth and it guided him well.

We packed all of his belongings and said good-bye to Pohaku. As we were driving home, Aunt Ruth commented that Pohaku seemed to emit a rare quality about him. She said that she felt an immediate attraction towards him.

We stopped by the house to drop off his belongings just as my mother was saying good-bye to a young soldier. Aunt Ruth remained in the car and I carried all of his things to his room without saying a word.

I closed the door behind me just as I heard my mother speaking in a voice half-heightened with satisfaction: "Oh, did ya git all 'o Andrew's things?" Linda came crashing through the door. Breathlessly, she remarked: "I just heard from Aunt Ruth outside about Andrew. Poor old Andrew, I know he is up there right now saying, 'Thank you God for getting me away from this old messed up family, especially that old woman.'"

We both unpacked his clothes and books and papers and as we were unpacking, she said, "You better take all of his papers with you because I know before the day is gone, she will have all of that stuff outside in the dumpster and burned up."

I put the papers back into the box and took them outside and loaded them into Aunt Ruth's car and we left.

On Saturday morning, at two minutes past ten, we attended a brief ceremony held at the hospital which was planned by Pohaku. Aunt Ruth drove Uncle Randy, Linda and me to the little chapel.

I don't recall who attended the services—my mother did and some more members of the family. I think James and Peter were there.

There was no coffin, just a brass urn and a portrait of Andrew on an alter. Pohaku spoke. And in a heavenly voice he said: "Let there be no sorrows, no griefs, no toils and cares. Our brother Andrew, who is more precious in the sight of God than any of us he has left behind, has left this fallen world and returned to the paradise of his Eden where he will dwell for eternity in peace and in purity."

Zoom!

Those words again, *Paradise*, *Eden*.

Was Andrew still speaking to me through Pohaku? Will Pohaku teach me where Andrew left off? He did say that Pohaku had some things to tell me before I left.

We left the chapel and negotiated the distance across the lawn towards the lake. It was a bright, clear and crisp autumn day. Across the lawn to our left, were some apples ripening on their branches as a soft gush of wind kissed them as they waved. On the hills across the lake, the shifting shadows of the autumn clouds moved towards us like the guardians of the place and stopped just above us.

In the valley below the hills rich with flowers; the ripening harvest of corn and pumpkins guarded by a brilliant row of evergreen hedge; the verdant pastoral sweeping grass; the acorn trees; the maple and evergreen; the clustering vines; the curious squirrels; beavers and chipmunk and the raven and the robin were all there to say good-bye.

In the distance could be heard the life and gladness of childish laughter peeling forward as we approached the edge of the water. Pohaku, without uttering a word opened the vase and scattered the ashes over the lake. The wind distributed them evenly as they drifted slowly downstream with the soft and sunlit smiles of God.

Fourteen

A New Heaven . . .

Aunt Ruth let me come and stay with her and Uncle Randy. I really liked living with them. Ronald was three years older than I and he sometimes treated me as though I was his younger brother, but I liked him and liked hanging out with him. He was an excellent student and never doubted for a second that he would not attend Harvard when he graduated from high school. He finished cum laude and was admitted to Harvard and from there he had all of his sights set upon becoming a medical doctor.

I studied him carefully and admired his certainty and determination. I'm positive that the small amount of time that I spent with him and his family, contributed to my growth and development ten thousand times more than the times I spent in the stagnated and decaying atmosphere in my home and with my family.

Aunt Ruth was a sober, silent, handsome, elegant, and queenly woman. She was alive, alert, receptive, and still discovering. Her face showed experience, but not extreme age. The corners of her mouth were not turned down, her eyes were not dimmed, and her face showed no signs of wrinkle. Although she attended the Baptist church, she was not a fervent religious saber rattler.

I was very fascinated by her un-Christian style and demeanor. She and Ronald didn't attend church regularly, and I don't believe Uncle Randy ever attended. I asked him why he didn't go to church and he replied, "Church is good for those who need it."

My greatest joy in living with them was because I could discuss my thoughts with them freely and wholly without any fear of retribution. For the very first time in my life, I felt completely free. Totally Free! Free as Adam! And, to add to this blessing, I really felt that they loved me as I loved them. This was paradise for me.

I was never envious of Ronald because he was so well blessed. I enjoyed his blessings just as much as he. And although our lives scattered us to the far corners of the earth, I was always welcomed to his home and without any conditions. My brothers James and Peter were the only Broomfields which shared this same relationship with me.

A few weeks after Andrew's death, I called Pohaku and asked if I could come up and visit. He was delighted to hear my voice and I became as excited as he in anticipation of our meeting. My visits with Pohaku were not restricted to weekends as they were with Andrew, so we decided that Wednesday evening would be best. In preparation for the meeting, I re-read Andrew's material and the Book of Genesis.

I arrived at six o'clock at Pohaku's and he had prepared a meal for us. I entered his building and proceeded down the hallway to his room and looked across the hallway to Andrew's room. It was occupied with an elderly gentleman from Poland whom Pohaku said was a bit confused as to which world he was actually living in.

Pohaku could speak several languages. He once told me that he really didn't know just how many languages he actually spoke. He said that he didn't think in terms of different languages. For him, there was only one language and he could converse with people anywhere, even with inhabitants living in the remotest parts of the world.

We sat and I devoured the meal he had prepared. It was a delicious offering of the most scrumptious clam chowder soup in the universe. I have never been able to find another mixing of chowder which topped his. After we finished our meal, Pohaku said that we would use the processes of autonomic thought to look at some rather perplexing questions he thought were pertinent for my growth and development.

He was a master of time management and without much hesitation he began to speak. His opening words were fascinating:

> To begin, the first business of opening the mind to AT to learn God's will is to begin at page one of nature and to get an understanding of the laws of Creation.
>
> Your brother Andrew gave you a rather good description of autonomic thought and so in this first session I'm going to take you to law school. Okay?
>
> Do you think you can handle it? Of course you can.

"Yes, I think so," I replied in a rather sheepish tone. He continued:

> As our understanding of these laws begin to unfold, we will see that they are not only as perfect as their Creator who established them, but they are also perfect for

all of its creations which is nature.

Also, since nature is perfect in all of her operations, so will her products be perfect since this is the same relationship which exists between her and her Creator. Follow me?

"Yes? I think so."

I just want to go back to our earlier discussion when we were talking about who came first. Do you recall that conversation?

"Unh Hunh."

Well, you will recall that it was my contention that the seed of the woman preceded the man in the scheme of all creation. If we study the real subtleties that authors have traditionally written and as we have been taught, you will notice that we refer to nature as "Mother Nature"—which you will see in our discussion, is where all life originated. Keep this in mind as our discussion progresses and as we point to the interrelatedness of relationships and the laws which govern them.

Since there is this harmonious relationship between the Creator and nature and its products, then there is a harmonious relationship between nature and the products it produces. This applies to both the animal and the vegetable kingdoms. A formula could be constructed: Creator + harmony = Nature + harmony = Products (animals, vegetables; physical, mental) ad infinitum.

I will explain these in more detail by way of giving you a set of laws which governs these relationships. Again I remind you that this discussion may appear to be rather complex at times and I want you to stop me at any point of the discussion that you don't understand.

Let's begin with the first law, the **law of identity** and its co-agent the **law of transmission**. Sometimes I will refer to this same law as the law of correspondence. A simpler way of saying this is **"like produces like."** This law is the result of nature being in harmony with the Creator's expectations to execute its will. We do not know what the Creator's "will" is except as it is manifested to us through demonstrations. And we still have no real understanding of its authenticity.

This law of identity also applies equally to both the animal and vegetable kingdom. This equal application to both kingdoms is included in both of their intellectual departments.

"What do you mean by that. Are you saying that vegetables have intelligence?"

I'm saying that the same vital principles which preserve the animal kingdom is also preserved in the vegetable kingdom. For instance, there is no evidence to show that when a child is born the Creator created a new soul to accommodate the body.

It is just a matter of the law of transmission which accommodates the identity of the new child's soul with the soul of its Creator. It is a continuation of the soul and identity of the Creator. Recall: 'I and the Father are one?'

Just as there is no evidence that when a new vegetable is produced that it is not a result of this same progressive law of transmission from the seed. No new seed soul is created by its Creator to accommodate the ear of corn produced by the corn seed.

What I'm trying to say is; there was just as much God in the universe when there was just one man and one ear of corn as there is right now in this universe with its billions of people and ears of corn.

Perhaps another example would be illustrative. Take a drop of water from the ocean and you will find that there is just as much ocean in that drop of water as there are drops of water in the ocean. The very same chemical properties exist in that single drop as in the entire ocean. You didn't have to create another ocean to accommodate this drop nor would it be necessary for future drops.

This is the underpinning principle of the operation of God and its relation to the universe. It has not changed one iota since its beginning.

"Still with me?"

"I think so."

Let me be a little more profane, just think of it as your blood line; your connecting link, your umbilical cord. Okay? Let's continue.

Since these laws are applicable to both kingdoms, and they are also immutable and their secrets are known only by the Creator, then the expectation of their results by the original Creator must correspond. Otherwise, there would be constant chaos and confusion.

For instance, when you plant a seed of corn you expect to harvest an ear of corn—not a tomato. And so the expectation by you, was an ear of corn. And you planted it and let the immutable laws of the Creator who only knows the secrets to these laws, make the seed grow into an ear of corn. So you leave it alone. You don't dig it up each day to see if its growing. It'll never grow if you did. You just leave it alone.

And this brings us to our next law—the **law of reproduction**. The same principals are equally applicable here for both kingdoms.

The same relationship between the seed and the soil and the child and the mother exist here as well.

For instance, a seed of corn is planted into the soil in which it fertilizes; germinates; is nurtured with ingredients from the soil; receives warmth and moisture; and with the same expectations and characteristics we had intended when we planted it, we get an ear of corn.

This identical process is applicable to the human, i.e., the seed of the mother; fertilization of the male for germination; nurturing in the mother's womb; moist and warmth; and with the same expectations of the sexual partners, a child is born.

Do you get it?

"Sure do. This is quite interesting."

But that isn't all. We have another law. Its the **law of perpetuity**. This law is to ensure that the identity, characteristics, and expectations of the Creator is maintained from generation to generation.

The co-agent to this law is the **law of cause and effect**. This is the law which causes the most conflict and difficulties because it carries with it contingencies which may modify a product. For instance, you will come to see that all water is not ice. Some water is ice. But all ice is water. The confusion begins when you tarry in your understanding of this little syllogism and adopt a belief that all water is ice when it really isn't so.

We'll get more involved into these laws and show their application to the Adam and Eve story. But before you leave tonight I want to speak a little bit more about what Andrew said to you regarding the Adam's 'who's on first' scenario.

Given our discussion tonight, and looking at the laws of nature and the establishment of the progressive expectation of the Creator, you should be able to deduce from this that the seed of the woman had to precede the male. This is because the expectation (potential) of the Creator had to precede the product, and for the final product to become manifest, it had to adhere to all of the laws in order to progress.

It was beginning to get a little late, and Pohaku had put a lot on my plate tonight for me to digest, so I left with these thoughts buzzing in my mind. I went straight to bed and couldn't close my eyes all night.

One word kept coming to my mind as I laid there, "Damn! Damn!" I thought to myself **AT** certainly isn't easy, that's for sure. No wonder so many people use supplanted thought—all they have to do is memorize things or just follow orders.

As Pohaku spoke about planting the seeds and the new souls not being created when a child is born, an old memory flashed back to when we planted our little private gardens at the orphanage.

I would dig a little plot of land and plant seeds of beans, corn, watermelons, cherries, peaches, and apples—all of the things I liked. I planted them in separate rows, but I also must have accidently dropped a few corn seeds on the ground close to close to the garden. I watered and tended my garden daily.

Shoe had a little plot not too far away from mine, so did Cornrows. They planted mostly beans, and corn and okra and squash—things of that sort. They never came to look at their gardens more than one or two times a week.

Sometimes Cornrows never showed up to attend his garden and so the weeds took over. Shoe would come and water his garden and take out the weeds. I watched every little green sprout which peeped its head from beneath the soil—each day a new sprout.

Some of the beans and corn came up within a matter of days. The cherries and apples and peaches and all of the other good stuff didn't, especially the watermelons. I became anxious and curious why the melons hadn't sprouted, so I dug up the seeds to investigate.

The seeds looked as if they had died and so I was disappointed and threw them away. After a few days had passed, I saw a little sprout breaking the soil in the spot where I thought I had removed the melon seeds.

I was curious and so I dug it up. It was the seedling of a watermelon with roots and a stem attached to the shell of a watermelon seed. I looked it over very carefully and put it back into the ground. The next day it had begun to wither. I watered it until its roots surfaced and I stuffed them back into the ground. All of these efforts were fruitless and the plant died.

One day as I was approaching my garden, I looked down and saw some vegetation growing where I had thrown the seeds, and it looked just like the watermelon seedling I once had in my garden.

There were also some plants growing in the weeds close to my garden which looked the same as the corn in my garden. I showed all of these marvelous discoveries to Shoe and he very casually said, "You should not mess with the garden after you plant the seeds. Leave them alone and let nature take care of them." His garden was booming with healthy plants. We looked at Cornrow's garden and it was just a patch of weeds. All of his plants were small and frail.

Following Shoe's advice, I left the garden alone, and the corn and beans were plentiful and the melons which grew "wild" after they were ejected from my garden, grew very large. Their vines spread all over the place, and we had watermelons for days. The cherries and the peaches and apples never did grow.

Pohaku's comments about the soul also made me think of the little kitten I found and my attempts to become a cat owner. We were strictly forbidden to own any pets at the orphanage even though the Peays owned two dogs themselves. But one day as I sat watching the garden, I heard this little faint sound "meow" coming from the bushes. I went to where the sound was coming from and looked into the frightened eyes and pleading cries of a little grey kitten.

I picked him up and he scratched me, so I threw him down. He didn't go away. He just stood there crying, "meow, meow."

"Alright," I said to myself, "you must be hungry." I sneaked into the kitchen and stuffed some cold biscuits and grits into my pockets and put them in front of the cat to eat. He wouldn't eat it so I asked, "What is wrong with you, where did you come from, where is the mother cat?"

Shoe, who had walked up behind me without me noticing him, said, "She's around here somewhere. That cat don't want that stuff, kittens want milk."

First of all, his silent approach behind me scared me nearly to death, and the fact that the cat's mother could be close by and could come and bite me for throwing down her kitten made me even more frightened. He said wait til I come back, and he scooted off to the kitchen.

He returned with a jar full of milk and sat it down before the kitten and it just lapped until it was all gone. I looked at Shoe with the biggest grin on my face, while at the same time wondering, "Where did he get all this knowledge from. Who told him about this? I've known him since from the first time we met in diapers."

Shoe left me sitting under my favorite oak tree with the kitten folded in my arms sleeping and purring. I sat there with him until it was time for us to go in for the night. I wanted to keep the kitten. I couldn't bring him into the house and hide him in my bed, which I had thought of doing. I had no place to hide it.

A "brilliant" thought came to me; dig a hole and place something over it so he wouldn't escape. I dug a hole and placed a piece of glass over it so I could see him. I then packed dirt around the edges of the glass and put a big rock on top of it.

All night long, I thought about it. I thought about what name to give it, and should I share my secret with my special friends like Leyla, Deedy, Echols, Cornrows, maybe Joe Lewis, and of course my sister. Shoe already knew.

At daybreak the following morning after, we were given the permission to get out of bed; to wash up for breakfast; comb our hair and do our chores before being allowed to go outside to play. When all of these burdens were completed, my feet hit the ground with breath-taking speed, and within a flash, I was under the tree removing the rock; scattering the dirt; lifting the glass; and reaching for my kitten.

It was motionless. Its eyes were closed as if it were asleep. I

A New Heaven...

shook it to awaken it. It didn't move. I patted it—and still no movement. Shoe came and kneeled beside me and I handed it to him and he said, "He's dead."

"Dead? What do you mean dead? How come he's dead? Who could have killed him? Nobody knew where he was. The glass, the dirt and the rock had not been moved. How did he die?"

Shoe asked me where did I put him last night.

"Right there," pointing to the hole.

"You mean you put him in the hole?"

"Yes, and I covered him with the glass and packed dirt around it and put this rock on top of it."

He looked at me in amazement as he raised his voice, "You dummy, you buried the cat alive."

"I did what?"

"No wonder he died. He couldn't get any air."

"I put the glass over it so he could get some air."

"That was not enough air. Air don't go through no glass. Charlie, I thought you knew this. You are real smart in school, but you don't seem to know nothing when it comes to these other things."

I sat there and cried until my eyes became dry. And, then another "brilliant" thought came to me, "'Cats have nine lives! This is only a kitten, so he must have eight more lives."

I placed him on a tree stump covered with my rag-handkerchief. There he would remain until he "came back to life." I was relieved by this thought, as I recalled the Easter Story when Jesus came back after three days.

I wouldn't go near the spot until after three days. When the three days had passed, I went to see it and it had begun to smell. There were lots of big blue-black flies swarming over it.

I was horrified. I chased the flies away and dug another hole and placed him there and became embittered about the nine lives. I was too embarrassed to tell Shoe, so I kept this all to myself.

This incident spurred me into thinking about the soul and God and where did the kitten's soul go to. And if God had to create eight more souls for the other eight lives, or was it just a bunch of lies.

Anyhow, Pohaku rekindled my thoughts during this session and like Andrew's discussions, I could hardly wait until the next one.

Fifteen

And A New Earth . . .

I had been talking to Aunt Ruth and Uncle Randy about the discussion with Pohaku. Uncle Randy was interested in the concept, but Aunt Ruth was very intrigued with it. She wanted to know as much as she could about it because she said that she and my daddy used to talk about things like that when they were growing up together.

I was really thrown for a loop when she asked me if I would ask Pohaku if she might join us in our discussions.

WOW! REALLY?

My chest stuck out like a proud peacock when at my next meeting with Pohaku, I asked if it would be all right for her to join us.

"Yes of course she is most welcome to come. Feel free to bring anyone else you think would be interested." Oh boy, now I was really excited.

He didn't waste any time before delving right into the discussion. He began by cautioning me that this time we might be moving into some areas which have not been fully developed in the understanding of humans and have caused quite a bit of conflict and controversy. He also said that it would be a rather lengthy discussion and he hoped I had come prepared to expend some "extra" cerebrum energy:

As we left off last time we said that **like produces like**, that's a natural law. Right? But contingencies may modify how things may appear to us, yet all of the laws of identity, transmission, and perpetuity are maintained. These laws apply to the mental and intellectual parts of the mind as well as its physical manifestation.

Listen carefully to my next remarks. You've no doubt heard people say to you that 'you look just like your dad or mom or you act like one of them,' right? Why do you think this is so?

Before I could attempt to give an answer, he continued his remarks and began to answer himself.

You might not be fully aware of the fact that the condition of the mental and intellectual energies of the parents at the time of conception will transmit to the offspring which will correspond with that which predominated at the time of conception.

If the parents, at the time of conception, are really excited to an inordinate degree, the baby will receive the characteristics of the parent which predominated at that time.

Family resemblance is governed by this law of identity. The law of transmission carries its moral characteristics such as the intellect and then the physical also becomes established.

Additionally, the mind of the mother exerts influence on the fetus during the time of gestation. Since this is the case, then an argument could be made that parents should be held responsible for the influence which they exert on their offspring.

I will say to you as a beginning thought, that if a child is born prone to doing "evil," it must be in this way and only in this way.

"Why?" I asked becoming very skeptical in my acceptance to this statement.

This may sound a bit confusing to you but I'll explain in more detail during another discussion. It is because God who is good, cannot **directly** create a being which is opposite to its own characteristic and at the same time be consistent with himself and deal justly with his creations by inflicting punishment upon them for their opposition. Keep in mind the word "good" when we have our discussion later.

Adam did not beget children in the likeness of his Creator, but in the likeness of **himself.** Why? You might ask. It was because the conduct of Adam modified the natural tendencies and predisposition of **his** son, and the conduct of **his** children modified the tendencies or governed the predisposition of **their** children, and so it goes right on down the line to us.

The puzzled look on my face increased as he continued:

I know you are still pondering about this, and so are the greatest minds there are. These are the foundations which we will develop as we discuss its applicability to the Adam and Eve story and their reconciliation with the Creator. Okay? Our first question then becomes, 'Does nature ever deviate?'

Our first answer to our first question says '**No.**' However, these laws of nature may be modified, but only with contingencies as I pointed out to you just a minute ago. Lets look at something that strikes fear in many people in this country—interracial marriage of a Caucasian and an African-American.

If the Caucasian should for five successive generations have children of the offspring of the African-American, every trace of the African-American, as it relates to color would disappear.

There will also be a modification of the features as well, and the same would be vice versa. The Caucasian complexion would become eradicated and its features would be modified. However, the law of identity would not be violated.

Now, in compliance with what I just said, let us say for purposes of discussion that God created Adam and Eve and placed them in Paradise to be governed by the laws He had established, while at the same time giving them the power to follow their natural tendencies and to modify them as circumstances arose in order that they might be responsible for their decisions and their actions. We'll analyze this in more detail later.

These rules included the laws of nature as well as His external rule to direct their human conduct. In doing so, God left them with the power of choice. They had to choose whether they would or would not select for their guide, their natural tendencies as humans to express the will of God. Or, would they obey the external 'Thou shalt not' command given by God. Or, if they would ignore the verbal command and go with their natural tendencies as directed by the laws of nature. Their future depended upon what choice they would make. It was a tough call.

Now let's look at this a little bit closer.

If the criteria given to them was equally balanced to make the choice, then they should be held responsible for their decision.

Then you might ask, 'What about contingencies or motives?'

Well, if equal motives were presented to them for them to decide, they are also held responsible. But, if the criteria and motives were not equally balanced, this formed the basis for a conflict between their natural tendencies and the demands made upon it.

The motives they were confronted with included curiosity on Eve's part and love for Eve on Adam's part. These motives then, tipped the balance which caused them to act in disobedience to God's will.

Aristotle was a bit more generous than God in his treatment of what constitutes a good act as opposed to a bad act in his Nicomachean Ethics, which stated that you should weigh the preponderance of good versus that of bad in an act in your declaration as to whether it was a good act or a bad act.

God tipped the scales in His favor so He could solicit their obedience to Him. He gave them a superior test by proclamation in an audible manner: 'Thou shalt not.'

Now, don't be too quick to start pointing the finger at God. He intended that man should be happy **but only as far as the development of his (man) character would permit.**

I underscore this very crucial point because you will see its relevancy in all of your future relations, both personal and religious. **You will receive happiness or satisfaction in all of your encounters <u>only</u> up to the point of your understanding.**

Additional happiness is extended to you as additional understanding is gained by you. This is the way in which you develop your character. I think Andrew had begun this discussion with you just before he died. Let us look at this a little closer. Andrew stated that God cannot do any more for you in the future than what He is doing for you right now.

God was faced with this same situation with Adam. Even the Creator could do for Adam only what Adam could do for himself. For God to give him perfect happiness to begin with and at the same time to have him to develop his character fully which might also include finding happiness, i.e., to have man a free agent and responsible for his acts is impossible even for the Creator.

The decree given to Adam as well as the other animals that "Thou shall do. . ." presupposes that they were properly equipped to perform under all circumstances and was a license to pursue all of the natural predispositions of their nature. However, the decree that "Thou shalt not do. . ." was a command of restraint. Therefore, if Adam did not possess the ability to do or not to do under all circumstances when he was created, he was not a free agent in situations which would involve him in very critical situations. The case with Adam was his yielding to the solicitations of his companion and face death or rebuke her and live. By the way, Homer and Shakespeare have made millions of happy readers by capturing this very same dilemma in their literature.

But I ask you, how could God have done otherwise without making Adam an automaton or a slave? My answer is: He could not create man with a free will and a responsible being with a character to be developed and at the same time leave him passive or indifferent to the influences of situations as they may arise. For instance, when you glance at an object of beauty, your natural tendency would be to respond in a positive if not aggressive manner to either share its beauty or acquire it.

I was getting a little confused so I asked him if my understanding of what he just said was correct. I stated, "I think I understand you saying that God was sort of caught up in some kind of a dilemma. You said that God could not have created human and given him perfect happiness and still obey the laws of nature.

"You're half right but your answer jumps over a lot of uncovered territory, but go on."

"And so God could not make man with his natural tendencies already fully developed and expect him to be responsible for his decisions and actions. Neither could he make man a free agent and yet punish him for whatever actions man might choose. Wow! God was in a pretty tight spot right from the beginning. Correct?"

Correct enough but let's continue and maybe we'll find an answer to this dilemma. Now listen carefully. The fact that Adam could have acted contrary to his natural predisposition is evidence that he already possessed all of the elemental principles of responsibilities of his being a free agent, he just didn't know it. It also shows that his **understanding**, not his **predisposition** should be held responsible for his act. The fact is that moral obligation is measured by what a man **knows** or **believes** to be either right or wrong, not his **predisposition.** Simply because you are predisposed to resist the color purple, does not give you license to dispose of everything purple.

So why did God infuse this element of discord with His verbal command? We'll have the answer to this question later during our discussion concerning the various tests God implemented with the pair. Okay?

"I think so. But I must admit it is a little bit complicated. I think I got the gist of it though. But go on. I like it very much." Pohaku seemed to be wrestling with a lot of information on his mind as he switched to what appeared to be another point he wanted to make. He was very thorough in all of his presentations and would not leave a subject without restating it at least two or three different ways so that he was satisfied that I got the message. He continued:

If it is true that the mind of man is controlled by the principles which are in harmony with his physical development; and if it is true that the moral nature of man can be so easily changed merely by one single act of volition in disobedience to a verbal command, it must also be true that these modifications may be whimsically transferred from one generation to the next. And since these modifications are based upon contingencies which emanate from cause-and-effect, man is free to act as he chooses—then all of God's creations would be for naught. Right? Well, lets see.

I say to you, man now possesses the same elementary principles as Adam and Eve, and the differences of our development from his may be found in the conditions we find ourselves in. If Adam and Eve are to be taken as a standard for which man relates to his Creator, then man should yield to the impulses of the laws of his nature rather than yield to the will of his Creator. As I said earlier, this 'thou shall not' command only set the stage for temptation.

A predisposition to do either good or evil depends on its relations to temptation. The fact that the natural tendencies of man may be directed towards either virtue or vice, depends entirely upon the influences which may be brought to bear on his mind at that particular time. For Adam it was simply a bite of the fruit.

Let me be more specific. For instance, if a most vicious individual is placed in a set of circumstances which favored the development of purity of his character, and we continued to work with that individual, in a few generations he would acquire the tendencies of purity and right.

The doctrine of redemption confirms this. It teaches that all which is required of man is to give his heart to God, in other words, to change the object of his supreme affections. He is not required to pick up any new attributes or possessions, but just to obey his Creator.

This doctrine, used as a means to restore man to the moral condition of purity, only means a restoration or a new direction towards the primary condition which Adam possessed before his "fall" and was pronounced by his Creator to be "very good."

Later in our discussion I will give you an extended view of Adam and his primary condition before the "fall." I want to talk more about this topic but I know this is a heavy session for you, however it is very important for you to know this in order for you to have a complete understanding of this whole topic.

Let me just say this; if the Creator of Adam created his natural tendencies at the time when He established His "thou shalt not" test in order to develop his character, God acted needlessly, because if Adam was a sinner when he was introduced into this world, such a test of his character was uncalled for because he must have already possessed a tendency which was hostile to its will. And if the Creator knew this was so, why construct a test to determine something which He already knew.

If Adam was brought into this world with a tendency which was in conflict with the will of his Creator without his knowledge or consent, then I ask you, how did he get it? Where did it come from?

If Adam had no knowledge of the conflict, should he be held responsible for yielding to the dictates of his nature even though he might displease his Creator when he had no other guide for his conduct. If Adam was not at liberty, either to resist or to yield to temptation, he could not have possessed any virtue, because where there is no temptation, there can be no virtue.

Listen to this, man is no more responsible to reveal the will of God than the beasts of the field, or the fowl of the air, or the fishes of the sea, or the plants of the field.

The development of the Creator's will, will harmonize with all grades of the intellects in which his products possess. A mother bird is no less caring for her offspring than a human is for hers. The beauty of the flowers are no less charming than the canvas of the artist; the song of the nightingale is no less beautiful than the harpist; the grace of the dolphins is equal to the ballerina; and the pastoral habitat of the wild beasts is no less charming than urban blight.

If Adam, as a representative of the human family, brought into this world death with all our woes as a consequence to his hostile nature or condition towards his Creator, then God committed the original sin. How could God have pronounced him as very good?

However, if Adam was brought into this world to receive a just retribution for his past offenses against his Creator, he must have been a sinner in a previous state of being, consequently the expression "very good" could not apply to him with any degree of consistency, justice, or right, nor would it either be just or right to inflict punishment upon his children without informing them why they were punished any more than it would be to have dealt so with their parent Adam. I ask you, does not the expression "very good" when spoken by the Creator imply perfection?

This declaration from the Creator would have never been announced if there had been one iota of Adam's nature in conflict with His will.

Furthermore, if Adam did not transmit to his children the elements of their character, as well as the peculiarities of their mental characteristic, who did? If it be possible for man to acquire a propensity to do evil and transmit the same to his offspring, who should be held responsible for the offspring's tendencies—man or his Creator?

If it should be that it isn't possible for man to transmit to his offspring such evil tendencies, and at the same they are ushered into this world with such depraved tendencies, where should the responsibility rest to rebel against this doctrine of total depravity? It certainly cannot be injustice upon the offspring because he had nothing to do with it in either word or deed and his tendency was imparted upon him without his knowledge or consent.

It is important to note that identity of character cannot be maintained without the exercise of memory. If a man does not know where he came from, he certainly can't determine where he is going. He who would inflict punishment upon a subject, and not let him know the specific charges of guilt preferred against him, must be a tyrant.

As God is just in all His dealing with His creatures, will He not vindicate His justice by exonerating the offsprings from all responsibility which the parent incurs? If parents love their children, will they not try to make them happy by setting up guidelines to govern their behavior? And, will they not explain to the children the reasons for these guidelines and try everything they could to have the children follow these guidelines?

If this is so, then how could it be true or just that the Parent who loves mankind should make him suffer for something that he is totally ignorant of? Haven't we been taught that *God is more merciful than man?* Can He act this way simply because He has the power to do so?

I said previously that the relationships that exist between parents and their off-springs should harmonize with those which exist between the Creator and the parents. Both God and parent obligations should be reciprocal and based upon justice. Both are under equal obligations to promote the welfare of those who are without their knowledge or consent, brought into this world dependent upon them for protection, guidance and happiness.

Certainly, man today is no more responsible for what Adam did more than six thousand years ago any more than Adam for whatever may have occurred to him six thousand years before him.

Pohaku was on a roll. He was pacing to and fro without missing a beat and not seemingly searching for a word or a thought. It seemed as if he was not speaking these words, that they were somehow coming through him from someplace else and he was just a channel for them to flow through.

I soaked in every word and meaning he said and was engrossed with his articulation and depth. At one point I felt myself also anticipating and speaking the words with him, so it was not a difficult session for me. My mind seemed to have expanded beyond my years in my comprehension of what he was saying. I sparkled with enthusiasm as Pohaku kindled new embers of understanding in me.

As he looked at my childlike fixation, he stated:

I will give you some interrogatories for you to take with you so we can have an extended discussion based upon these at our next meeting. I ask you to look at the following questions:

1. If the intellect can decide contrary to the will, which of them should hold man accountable for his acts?

2. If two individuals act contrary to each other by the influences of the will regardless of their understanding, which of them would be acting right according to the standard of moral obligation?

3. How can a man be a free agent and yet does not possess the power to deviate from his natural tendencies when temptation presents inducements to disregard them?

4. What could Adam have known of good or evil while yielding to the inclinations of his nature as established by his Creator?

5. If Adam could appreciate the relationship between cause and effect and could yield to the strongest inducement, how could he have refused to yield to the solicitations of his beloved Eve, and to share his destiny with her?

6. If the destiny of man depends on the freedom of the will and at the same time the will is controlled by contingencies which are beyond his control, would it be an injustice for God to hold man responsible for what he could or could not avoid or prevent?

Think about these and come prepared next time. I also am expecting that you will bring your aunt to our next meeting. As he said these words to me, they sounded as if there were a direction, not a request. I said I would ask her and felt mighty proud that he would even suggest it.

I scampered home to crow about the session. Aunt Ruth was in her study reading her Bible and invited me to join her. I told her that Pohaku had asked me if I would ask you if you were interested in joining us at our next meeting. "Of course, I would be delighted to. Now I can put this away where it belongs for awhile as I'm sure Pohaku will provide a proper guide for me."

She placed the Bible on the bookshelf and turned to me and asked if I could tell her about some of the things we had discussed. Although it was a long session with Pohaku, I was very happy to share our discussion.

We talked until well past midnight, when Ronald came home with an arm-load of books yelling, "Man, those people at Harvard don't think we have anything to do but read all of this nonsense they give out. I hope you're not thinking of going to Harvard. I didn't mean that as a put-down, I'm just looking out for your poor wretched soul, my man," then he disappeared into the refrigerator.

Aunt Ruth and Uncle Randy were quite interested in some of the things I would say to them. I told them practically everything that Andrew had said to me and they were saddened that they didn't get the opportunity to know him better.

No one except Linda seemed to have known him. He was just deposited in the hospital and left there. Before I started my visit, she would visit him and made sure that he had sufficient reading material. After living with Aunt Ruth, I could see some striking similarities between them. They were both free thinkers yet kept their own counsel. Neither of them would give unsolicited information, but if you asked them a question, or showed an interest, then they would go out of their way to satisfy your inquisitiveness.

Sixteen

About My Father's Business . . .

*W*ednesday evening came and Aunt Ruth drove us to the hospital in the big shiny Cadillac. I felt a bit uneasy in it when people began to stare at us, stoop down and peep inside or walk along the side of it as we drove slowly to the parking area. As she parked the car, there was a small throng of people following us. One man opened the car door for us and assisted Aunt Ruth out of the car. Another man asked if he could carry my book bag. I refused his offer.

This was all exciting as well as a bit unnerving to me. Aunt Ruth did not seem to be affected at all. She even had a brief conversation with two young ladies on her way through the building.

When we arrived at Pohaku's room, his Polish neighbor greeted us as if he had been expecting us and invited us to have tea and toast with him. I said, "No thanks."

But Aunt Ruth said, "Oh thank you, I would be happy to have tea with you, and bring him some as well, I'm quite sure he'll enjoy it." His eyes immediately brightened and a new spark of life seemed to energize him as he very sprightly marched

About My Father's Business...

across the hallway humming a Polish folk tune.

Pohaku extended his hand to her and greeted her while welcoming her to his "most humble little world." Within minutes, the neighbor was serving us tea, and Pohaku asked him if he wanted to stay and he said yes. We drank the beverage contentedly and I was overwhelmed by the thought that Aunt Ruth was here with me and that she liked Pohaku.

We all began to look towards Pohaku, and he seemed to have murmured a word to himself in some strange language before he settled into his lecture. Before he started to speak I blurted, "I studied all of the questions you gave me and I also went over them with Aunt Ruth and Uncle Randy."

Very good. They will be most useful to you. Now lets get started. We will begin by asking the questions:

What is our place in the universe? Why was man created?

By the way, I want to stress that my usage of the word 'man' has no gender attached to it. I only use it in the generic sense which includes both male and female. We had a previous conversation regarding the appearance of man on earth, but what does this all mean to us?

Let us look again at this name "man." It comes from the Sanscrit root **MN** which conveys the idea of measurement. This is in the same sense as the word "mind" is derived from the Latin **mens** which means to have the capacity to compare things, to see things in their relationship to another. Take a look at the heavenly body which we call the moon. The phases of the moon gives us the most obvious standard for the measurement of time. The menstrual cycle of the woman is a predictor of a "period" of time, and what is the root word that you see in the word "menstrual?" It is during this period that cleansing and the preparation of the regenerative forces take place in the woman—a period of future "seeing."

If you ever have the opportunity some day, you should visit a place in Rome called the "Holy See." This is a very interesting place indeed which is all under the control of celibate men, yet our sexual and moral conduct is brokered by these men of the Holy See.

The word "month" is thus measured by these cycles. But in spite of all of this historical precedence, it might surprise you that the largest unit of weight measurement in India is called "man." Man is therefore the "measurer."

So this raises the question: Why did God have to include humans in His creations? Was His ego so supreme that He wanted to see if humans could measure up to Himself? He already had created the beasts of the fields and fowls of the earth and fishes in the sea.

Why couldn't He just stop right there? Why man? Certainly there would have been more peaceful and environmental harmony in the world and the troubles and heartaches He has suffered by mankind would not have been as such. Would nature had been better off if He hadn't? The answer is positively **no**!

And so the rightful answer can be found in one word *intelligence*. Divine intelligence is what the Creator is all about. But, the word *intelligence* is not confined to the species of mankind. The vegetable and the animal kingdoms possess the same intelligent system as mankind. Otherwise they would have been extinct long ago.

We were given the words, 'you shall know the truth and the truth shall set you free.' These are not just a loosely string of words without meaning.

But how do we arrive at the truth? We do it by reasoning and searching and asking and finding and asking again and finding again and with each inquiry, we come closer and closer to the destination in which we are going. Some might refer to it as our cosmic urge.

So listen carefully to my words tonight and try to focus on our questions.

I said that we need to seek and to probe in order to move forward. This is our progressive tendency which is embedded in the natural law of transmission and is harmoniously connected with the law of posterity or longevity. It's an essential element in our growth development for if we do not progress and move forward, then we 'shall surely die.' I'm not speaking singularly of dying in the physical sense. We must have a progressive tendency in us to move on to the next stage of development.

Can't you now see the contradictions in the Adam story? They were told that if they did move forward and obtain new knowledge that they would surely die. But we'll get into that a bit later.

Now, I've just said that our progressive tendency is a characteristic of the natural laws of the human economy. This is proved by the progressive stages through which all humans pass before their characteristics become fully developed. The old sayings, *nature, unaided, fails* or *nature abhors a vacuum* are germane to our discussion.

There are some fables and Andrew pointed out to you, that there are seven stages mankind goes through during his pilgrimage here on earth. I don't know when our progress will end, only God knows. But to indulge in the idea of how far we will progress has been really intriguing and truly enchanting because mankind may progress for myriads of years.

You were taught in John 3:16 that God gave His only begotten Son. I agree with this, minus the sexism. However, I do say that God only begat one Son and is still begetting and improving that Son in you and I and everyone else to make Him whole and fully developed.

By doing so, we are made wholly **at-one** with God. And by removing the hyphen or separation, we become **atone** with God. This separation was imbedded in us from the beginning through ignorance and error. In order for unity with the Creator to occur, we must overcome this ignorance. However, we must not suppose that unity means uniformity. We can be separate, but never separated from each other. This is not a contradiction, but it is the reason for mankind's gross misunderstanding of one another.

Let me say this, then I'll conclude for the evening. Diversity in unity is very necessary for any sort of expression or progression. Once we grasp this idea of unity and progressiveness of life going on **ad infinitum**, we will see what boundless sets of possibilities open before us.

We then can see that life leads us on from one stage to another, unfolding as it goes, and to this unfolding, there is no end because it is our eternity finding ever fuller expression. As it finds fuller expression, it must find more and more suitable channels through which it can flow, however, the channels must be suitable.

But from our limited viewpoint, we can see for ourselves that as man passes through two successive channels or stages of existence, he can form some idea of what will be the condition of the next one. He must then say to himself at each stage, 'this, or something better' and there he must stop and learn all that 'this' has to offer, be it happiness, relationships, or what have you; and when 'this' becomes stagnation and regressive, he must move on to the next stage, or else he shall surely die.

Moreover, to assert that because all men are not happy in this world of continual change and progress and that this is due to some conflict between him and God is absurd, because happiness was not the only objective for which man was placed here.

If this was so, then there would be nothing but complete unhappiness. Happiness must be the result of progressive action by man, not by decree or proclamation. The greatest proclamation of happiness is the one which you give to yourself.

This brings us to another important question. Why didn't God create us so that we could not be perfectly happy and think only positive thoughts? Let me shock you by saying: Because he couldn't. There are some things which even God cannot do. What would you say if I told you that even God could not make two plus two either more or less than four? He cannot do anything that is in itself contradictory. This would be tantamount to what some people are saying that God is the author of both good and evil.

To say this is equivalent as saying that God is inconsistent with Himself and consequently that He is not only imperfect, but unjust. Let us correct this thinking and say God is the author of a **being** who became evil by transgression of His laws because the laws of God are based upon the principle of justice. This is all that **sin** is. If we say that God is the author of sin, how can He also be the author of good and evil, because these are in conflict with each other. Sin is separating or transcending the laws of God. It is only after this separation from the law that we call good and evil. Since good and evil are just relative terms, neither of them can exist disconnected from action, be it mental or physical, there must be some standard by which they are shown. What is considered good today could tomorrow become evil and vice versa. The marketers of our morality have effectively confused the difference between sin and evil and this should be cleared up.

However, on the other hand, if God has established a standard which He deems is good for the human character, and He refuses to reveal it for our understanding, it is He who sins the most.

I will speak to you further about this topic.

Wow, this is some heavy duty stuff I thought. I never would have thought of these things the way Pohaku is explaining them. It all made sense to me also. I was always taught that I was a sinner from birth, but that I could do anything I wanted to do up until I reached the age of twelve, then God would begin to hold me accountable for all of the misdeeds I did.

I couldn't help but to glance over at Aunt Ruth, to get her reactions to what was being said. She looked as if she was entranced in another space. Her eyes seldom blinked and she seemed to be oblivious as to what was going on around her. I hoped that Pohaku would say just a little bit more before calling it quits because I knew she was enjoying every bit of it. He kept on going:

If God had placed man in this world with his happiness fully developed by decree, he would have been as happy in his first stage of development as he would in his next stage or his previous stage, so where's the incentive to progress?

God decreed otherwise. And who knows but God how many stages or conditions it will require to fully develop our tendencies which were given to us by Him alone.

The Creator, being divine intelligence, placed intelligent beings and other products of nature in this world to make progressive order out of chaos.

Now listen to me carefully. The Creator is never without a witness. In order to **do**, you first must **be**. We can **do** only to the extent which we **are**. We cannot express powers which we do not possess. The Creator, possessing as He does, infinite intelligence, could no more exist alone in this universe than man could exist alone and be perfectly happy in this world, because the Creator like man, possess a social element of His character which, if it could not be satisfied, would take away the happiness of even the Creator Himself.

This social element which I just mentioned is the

passion of love. The Creator has it, so does man. If we take this passion of love and we should find that it has no object upon which to bestow its affections, it would be the same as if it never existed. Recall: Nature, unaided fails! **Love must have an object.**

Remember this and place it deeply within you so you will never forget it. I will devote an entire session on this topic alone in the future.

When a human loves God, he in turn is beloved. And as God loves man, it is reciprocated as long as that channel remains open and suitable and man remains in that place in nature which sustains his natural tendencies to love.

This natural tendency to love is expressed through intelligent beings God has placed among us to show us the light of science and wisdom. If this were not the case, the world would be dark, dreary, and chaotic and might very well be obliterated.

Read John 1:5. He tells us that the light shineth in the darkness, and the darkness comprehended it not. Jesus put it very clearly when He said this is the condemnation of the world, that light came to the world but men loved darkness rather than light.

Go home and continue reading John. You'll find chapter 3: 19-21 very interesting.

Let me go back to expand on the previous question I asked you. If it were possible to annihilate every being in the universe, without a possibility of creating others, do you think that God would be satisfied to stick around alone in all the splendor that He was able to create for Himself? I don't think so.

Let me bring it to you closer to home. If you had all of the money and power and possessions and nobody else had anything at all, would you be happy enough to keep it all to yourself for any extended or indefinite period of time and still declare yourself as happy? Certainly not.

And so the happiness or unhappiness which we see in this universe is not evidence enough for us to say there is some conflict between man and God. Doesn't the kind parent who loves its infant, correct it for its wrongdoing?

This does not mean that this correction is reflective of the parent's hatred for the child. It is vice versa, unless of course, extreme measures of correction are used by the parents. But the loving parents are still the parents of the child who is in rebellion and would not think of extreme measures.

If God, like the parents, approves and disapproves, He must be subject to the emotions of grief as well as pleasure and happiness. If we place any confidence in the Bible, we cannot deny the fact that man is the object of intense love and anxiety by the Creator.

However, the Bible is replete with the assertion that God used extreme measures of correction—the flood for instance. This is contrary to all of the natural laws and the will of the Creator. This oxymoron (reasoning) is no different than when a lover shoots and kills his beloved, and his reason for doing so was because he loved her so much.

God loves His children and as the prophet Amos pointed out: 'just as the shepherd takes out of the mouth of the lion, two legs, or a piece of an ear of one of his sheep, so shall the children of Israel be taken out of Samaria.'

My heart saddened as he said these things. I wondered if Mr. Peay loved us in spite of the brutal beatings he inflicted upon us. I couldn't think of a reason why he would not love us simply because we were orphans. I thought that through all of the fear, pain, and suffering he inflicted upon me, I still loved him, simply because he and Miss Pounds were all I had as parents.

I was reminded of the time when I was about five years old when we went to the county fair. This was the big event of the year for us. Although it was in the segregated South, we could go to the fair on the two days which were set aside for colored people to attend. I remember riding the big ferris wheel along with Deedy and Shoe with me in one seat. When the ferris wheel stopped and we came to the end of our ride, everyone got off and there were lots of people scrambling at the same time to get seats.

I was knocked down and was unable to get to the ground from the platform until it was cleared. During this confusion I became separated from Deedy and Shoe and I suddenly found myself alone. I didn't know what to do but just stand there and cry. I began to cry for Deedy, Shoe, and Joe Lewis. They were nowhere to be found. I then started to yell for Mr. Peay and Miss Pounds. I started to run while crying and yelling at everybody who passed me asking them, "Have you seen Mr. Peay? Please help me to find Mr. Peay.

Suddenly I heard my sister May's voice yell, "There he is." I dropped my candied apple and my cotton candy and ran as fast as I could and grabbed Mr. Peay and held on to his leg as tightly as I could. He scolded me for getting lost and said he would tend to me later when we returned to the orphanage.

It was a very long but informative session and I enjoyed every bit of it. I'm quite sure that Aunt Ruth did also. Pohaku then paused for a moment and spoke a few words in Polish to his neighbor who nodded in assent to what was spoken to him. He said this was a good point to stop for the evening, and he closed his eyes for just a second and uttered another strange word to himself before looking in our direction.

Aunt Ruth finally came back into our space and joined me in thanking him for such a good discussion. She shook his hands and as the two hands met I felt a sudden surge of a connected spark of energy zip through my body. It felt as if I had received the same divine declaration, "Well done my good and faithful servant."

We left the building and there was a small gathering of people just outside. One of the two girls with whom Aunt Ruth had spoken with earlier stepped out of the group and said that they were proud that we had come up to visit with them and for us to please come back soon. Aunt Ruth smiled and held her hand and said, "Yes, I will come back."

As we reached the parking area where the car was parked, two men were waiting there for us. They each opened the doors to the car for us while stating that they had stood watch over the car because it was such a pretty car. We thanked them and we drove off.

Words cannot describe the feeling of exultation I felt as we drove home. My chest was puffed with pride. I felt as if I had accomplished something really big. We didn't speak on the way home because Aunt Ruth was deeply engrossed in her thoughts and I didn't dare wish to disturb her. A few days later as I was on my way out, I heard her discussing our meeting with Uncle Randy. I didn't get all of what she was saying but I heard Uncle Randy reply, "It might be a good idea. How much do you think it would cost?"

She replied, "I don't know but I certainly would like to try it for once and see if it works. I'll call around and see if we can find a suitable space for it."

"Ah Hah! They are going to have a party," I thought to myself. "That'll be nice."

All during the week, Aunt Ruth was on the phone making calls to a lot of people—some with high stature and some with no stature. She was telling them about the discussion she had attended with Pohaku and would be calling upon them in the very near future for their support.

Seventeen

Upon This Rock . . .

Wednesday came and we were again greeted with our welcomers at Pohaku's. The two men stood guard over the car, Aunt Ruth spent a little more time chatting with members of the group and we went to Pohaku's room where we were met and were greeted by six more people he had invited to the discussion.

I said to myself, wow this is getting to be something big. The Polish neighbor served us tea without invitation and Pohaku began in his usual trance-like fashion:

> The question we will speak to tonight will address the issue of Adam's responsibility for his yielding to his wife Eve in accepting the fruit. But before we begin, as I promised you earlier, I want to go back and complete the discussion I began regarding Adam in his primary state before his "fall."
>
> This leads me to ask a few questions:
> - Suppose Adam had not yielded to temptation?
> - What would have been his basis for happiness?
> - How would his mental powers been developed?

Their first signal of progressiveness was that he and Eve possessed the mental powers to either obey or disobey the commands of their Creator. Up to that time they could not have known any other moral or intellectual pleasure than that which was derived from a stupid ignorance of what moral or intellectual enjoyment was because the only standard they had for happiness was obedience to the laws of their own nature.

They didn't know what morality was before their transgression, therefore they could not have had any moral development. Since they had no inducement to develop their intellectual powers, their happiness and development could not have been of an intellectual nature either. So their happiness must have been confined to that of a mere social nature. All of Adam's happiness was derived from the presence of his wife Eve, playing with the animals, as well as the attraction of the beautiful surroundings in the paradise of Eden.

If there had not been placed any restraints on Adam and Eve's natural intellectual faculty, not only their lives but the lives of their children would have been one complete panorama of monotonous repetitions. They would be without any idea of morality and no ability to discriminate between good and evil. Consequently, the animal instincts would have been the rule of action and they would be controlled by their passions and from motives purely sexual.

It is competition that inspires ambition because self-gratification awakens curiosity. We all feel the urge to vie with a competitor. So Adam and Eve were placed in competition with some prohibition in order that their ambitions, genius and skills might become aroused from their dormant state.

So what was the Creator's design to move Adam from this stupid state of intelligence to enable him to develop his character. I suggest that He set into being a test or its equivalent with criterion which would be by instituting a prohibition or restraint.

Wow! I saw where Pohaku was taking us with this discussion and I thought to myself; yes, he is right. The best way to get somebody interested in something is to say to them that they could not have something or do such and such. Something else also flashed in my mind as he was speaking: is this also where the expression 'curiosity killed the cat' came from. Did this come from Eve's curiosity, that she would die if she satisfied her curiosity by eating the fruit? Then he said something which threw me into a mental tizzy:

Amos, let me say this to you. I emphatically state that there is no fact, idea, or action of a moral nature without some sort of test by which an individual can determine whether he may or may not be justified in his actions or motives.

The tests the Creator instituted were the Law, the Prophets, (according to Hebraic tradition) and for the Christians, the Gospel. Briefly stated, the first epoch of the world demanded the Law for a criterion of development. The second epoch demanded a further test as the developments of his mental capacities became more expanded. There was then added the Mosaic Law the Pharasaic Law which was later canonized into the Mishnah which established a social order. Then there were the Prophets who advocated justice, Amos being the first to raise the questions of justice and equality during the third epoch.

The Gospel was then introduced which taught us redemption to meet the further expansion of the human character. We don't know what the test or criterion will be for the fourth epoch but I venture to say that it will soon become apparent to us since each of the epochs advanced in nearly equal number of years, two thousand each, to be exact. We are now close to the end of the two thousand year Gospel epoch.

There are some early signs which are beginning to show the next test. There appears to be a new ordering of the world into a community of nations. This is being spawned by the further advancement of the intellectual faculties. The advent of *intechnologence*, to coin a phrase, has begun to unite the world in such rapidity that it is now possible to accomplish in a second, what used to take require months or even years to do.

This was the first time he had called me Amos by name. And as he did so, my spine tingled with disbelief because when he first met me and Andrew introduced me as "Amos," it struck me with hardened clarity to learn that Amos was a prophet also and how Pohaku had begun to tell me about some of the things that would happen to me in my lifetime. Was Pohaku trying to tell me something? Am I going to be a prophet? I didn't feel like one. I wouldn't even know how to act like one. Pohaku was looking at me with a look which gave me a sense of uneasiness for the first time as he continued:

Let me just conclude this little discussion before we get into our topic for tonight by saying this: The distinguishing traits of the human character which slumbered in the primary condition of Adam and Eve became awakened by the *fall*. I urge you to look at Albert Camus in his discussion on the *fall*. To him, it was a *fall up* instead of down.

I conclude that mankind has now the same faculties that Adam and Eve had before the "fall" but the only difference is that these have been perverted by each succeeding generation of transmission. And to enumerate them would be useless.

But let us commence with our topic of discussion for tonight which is Adam yielding to the wishes of his wife Eve.

I begin, if he knew the consequences which would follow, and at the same time was willing to risk them, then he should be held responsible, **although he violated no law of his nature** which recognized the necessity of yielding to the strongest influences presented for his action.

Adam's natural tendency was so organized that it **should** render to the strongest inducement and yet his intellect, and not the passion, was the criteria which should guide his action. And so although he violated no natural law, he did refuse to obey the decisions of his intellect, and was therefore responsible. He knew it was not right because the intellect, and not the passions was authorized to make these moral distinctions.

But, it was as natural for Adam to love his Eve as it was for him to love his Creator, because this love was based on the harmonious relations which were given to him by his Creator. He was created with a predisposition to love a companion who was created for the consummation of his affection—and vice versa.

That's why they were created in the first place. And, I might add, without the companionship of woman, the world would be a curse to man. For man to be happy without a woman to be his companion would be an anomaly and therefore should be condemned. The loveliness of a woman is a blessing to man. The best entity in a home is a woman because she can grace it with loveliness, beauty, and affection.

Although Adam loved the animals, and as Andrew rather comically pointed out, God had to hurry and create an Eve for him to love.

But seriously, there was no more of a conflict between the designs of the Creator and the creation of Eve than there was between the creation of Adam and his Creator.

The relationship between the Creator, Adam, and Eve was harmoniously maintained up until the time Adam and Eve determined that it was time to reveal their relationship with each other. And, as I have said previously, the Creator is under just as much obligation to be just and fair to His creations inasmuch as the principles of justice can never be violated by either superiors or inferiors.

It was not natural or just for Adam to barter away his love for his wife for any consideration. His love for his wife was his strongest passion of his nature, as well it should be—to enjoy her companionship. This heroic decision was nature's long before it became contaminated by disobedience, or modified by contingencies.

Adam, while in the natural enjoyment of his wife whom he loved supremely, could not in the least be convinced that he would be happier by renouncing her for what he considered an uncertainty, even death, because he had no distinct idea of what that was.

Therefore, the love that he had towards his cherished companion Eve, was the most potent reason why he chose to refuse the demands of his Creator rather than be deprived of the happiness which would be given to them.

They concluded that if they could not be happy saints while separate, then they would be happy sinners together. This could have been the equivalent to the world's first divorce. So the question is asked; did God want to set this type of precedent? I think not.

Although it may be precedent setting by Adam that a man should cleave to his wife, this natural tendency is not peculiar to Adam and Eve. It has always been evidenced by all true lovers. There is no law against true love. This is taught to us by the authors of the Gospels.

Eve committed not evil. She was just as angelic and pure as Adam when she yielded to the tempter. She **meditated** no evil. The only motive she possessed was curiosity and, since motives, not acts characterize the moral qualities of all of our transactions, she did not wilfully betray her posterity for sin—she was deceived. The Apostle Paul has even stated this in her defense.

Curiosity, as we have seen, is a legitimate product of the progressive operation of natural law. Unless it can be gratified, it will never allow the person subject to it to be contented. Since it is controlled by contingencies, the impressions which are made on the mind must change what is already there and each new impression must have a harmonizing understanding or expectation with it. Eve's mind was impressed with the idea that if they ate the fruit it would qualify them 'to be as gods, knowing good and evil.' I ask you, what's wrong with that if we are made in God's image? Since neither Adam nor Eve knew the difference between good and evil, they yielded to the **means** by which they would know the difference, not the **effects**. Do you now see how the law of cause and effect can become troublesome by the supplanted thought process?

At this point, Mr. Milewski, Pohaku's neighbor, raised his hand and stated with a very soft smile on his face, "May I offer a suggestion and, if its all right with you folks, if we could stop right here and wait until next week and invite our friends to come and join us in our discussions, because this stuff is just too great for, I feel, just **us** to enjoy. I would like to share this good knowledge with others. How do you folks feel about it?"

Aunt Ruth said, "You know that was precisely what I had in mind and have been working all week on how we could do just what you suggested. I had thought that we could find a Hall or some small auditorium and use that as a meeting place and invite others to join us. I know quite a few people myself who would really benefit from these discussions."

Pohaku was standing next to one of the other participants in the room, she was showing him some notes she had scribbled on a tablet explaining that if we could meet someplace at the hospital, and meet with the people who have been standing outside waiting and listening to what was said, would be a great thing. Pohaku nodded his head in approval

I had no idea what some of the other discussion was about concerning supervisors and state officials and other preachers and how they felt. Pohaku asked us if this was something we really wanted to do, and if so, he would be willing to share his knowledge with everyone who was interested.

I don't know what it was, but something inside of me began to churn. It felt as if something big was in the air and it was about to happen and I felt that I was responsible for it. I couldn't discern if it was going to be good or bad.

I thought back to the time when Andrew and I began our own little conversations and we shared a lot of love during these discussions. I felt this same feeling in these meetings with other people but on a grander scale. I guess this was the feeling I was experiencing.

Aunt Ruth was able to get a room reserved at the hospital for our next meeting, but it took some arm twisting. She had several visitors to come to her house concerning this issue including the Mayor and the Assemblyman both of whom she knew very well and had been a substantial contributor to their political campaigns.

The phone was constantly ringing during this week. Uncle Randy was very cooperative and supportive. He even had a long and heated discussion with the preacher from the Baptist Church Aunt Ruth attended.

Uncle Randy was never one to bite his tongue on any

matter. I overheard him say to the preacher, "And that's the reason I don't go to church anymore. I know all of the scuttlebutt that goes on in there. You been preaching that same old garbage for years and ain't changed a bit. I know every sermon you done preached by heart. So why should I waste my time sitting up there and listen to you saying the same old thing over and over?

"And them same old ladies be just sitting there eating it all up. You be up there in that pulpit and start that old low-down moaning and groaning and shouting and yelling and spouting off a bunch of "one-liners" to try to impress us that you have read a few chapters of the Bible, and you start gyrating your behind and flexing your chest and flapping your wings like a rooster, and the ladies be standing there screaming and waving and yelling 'Hallelujah.'

"It ain't nothing more than a bunch of frenetic sexual foreplay between you and them. How many of them have you slept with? I've heard about at least three of them myself. You should be ashamed of yourself, you old coot. You almost fell off the chair one time and pretty near lost your voice remember? You better watch yourself. You're getting a little too old for that mess.

My wife still goes there every now and then, and I still give you my money to help support you, but you better get on the ball and get with this new stuff that people are now beginning to want to hear and to understand that it makes more sense to them, especially the young people. They are fast being converted to the idea that the same ole stuff you been dishing out for the last 40 something years don't make sense to them anymore."

The next week we arrived at the hospital and were greeted

at the gate by the security guard who was donning his habitual scowl which was quickly disarmed by Aunt Ruth's smile. His scowl quickly gave way to a toothless grin as he told us that the meeting was to be held in Emerson Hall which was situated next to the lake. It was a beautiful 19th century ivy-covered red brick structure with white trimmings.

We parked the car and walked into the building and were met by the Chief Administrator of the hospital who had little to show for his "high integrity." He was fat, flustered, red-faced, and with the look of a diabetic monk wearing a simian smile.

There were several muscular attendants milling back and forth; at least twenty or thirty. Faint sounds of the jingling of keys, the creak of heavy doors, and the click of secret locks could be heard in the background.

We entered the room and was I ever surprised. The room was completely filled with all sorts of people. There must have been at least 100 people in the room. Many of them were dwellers at the hospital who sat very quiet and obediently in their seats. Others were towns people and friends of Aunt Ruth.

Ronald had said he would skip one of his classes at Harvard and join us. He brought three students with him. It was very exciting. I was very happy. It was extremely rewarding to be included in this group.

Pohaku started the meeting by distributing his attention among the people in attendance. When the meeting was over, he did the same thing, and with amazing accuracy, he remembered each person's name.

Aunt Ruth was busy greeting her friends. Her social dexterity was something to watch. In a very short period, she had established her position as an intellectual leader of the group.

As I stood there watching her, I felt someone tap me on my shoulder from behind. I turned and looked straight into the eyes of a photo copy of Eve. She opened her mouth and immediately there was a twang of familiarity in her voice which eluded me.

"Hello, I'm Shirley. You probably don't remember me, but I met you at your mother's house sometime ago when you were talking to your mother and sister about God and Jesus. I look a little different now, don't I."

"Different! That's hardly the word for it. You look simply gorgeous." Just as soon as I said it, I realized how corny it sounded. I almost stumbled over my tongue trying to find something more apropos. I couldn't.

My only recourse was to revert back to my Adamic stage and internally shout at the top of my voice, **"Wah La Woo Wah, Oooh Wa La Woo!"**

I stepped back from myself and saw me do a little two step shuffling of my feet; rubbing my eyes; slapping my face; dusting my hair, and said, "Of course I remember you. I have thought of you quite often and, of course they have all been good thoughts. How is your work going?"

"Oh, I'm no longer doing missionary work. I stopped that soon after I heard what you had to say. I was only doing that because my stepmother made me go with her. She didn't want me to go out there sinning at my very young age."

"How old were you then, when I saw you?" I asked.

"Sixteen."

"What? I thought you were at least twenty five. I must have been around fourteen or fifteen."

"Naw, I was sixteen years old. I guess it was the way I was dressed."

I beamed!

I gazed into her "across the coffee table, formless grey dress wearing eyes" and thought to myself; I always liked girls older, younger, same age as me, pretty, luscious, witty, sassy, charming, graceful, exquisite, sophisticated, patient, refined, assertive, sexy, sensual, affectionate, lustful, voluptuous, salacious, and not related to me.

The trance was broken when Aunt Ruth called the meeting to order and introduced Pohaku. He had never looked more like a university professor than that evening. He had a look of a man with a sense of appreciation for art, science, and an emerging spark of intellect. His disposition displayed a man who could easily criticize his environment (instead of accepting it) while loving it at the same time. He turned away from the audience and muttered a few strange words to himself and began to speak:

This evening I will speak about matters of the heart and about love. Lets look at love first. And some of the things I say tonight will strike a familiar chord with all of you I'm sure, but I want you to hear it again for the first time.

Love is the tuning fork of life. It is one of man's natural tendencies given to us by God. Nothing is impossible to love but, we must be clear of the element of selfishness when we love.

Jealousy is an extremely difficult element to love and is always selfish. It is the root of most domestic strife. It claims to be the evidence of affection. It hides behind connubial concern, when it is nothing but schematic control which craves for ways to show its power.

Our love draws unto itself its corresponding quality

of affection. Love never needs to seek. If we make ourselves loving and lovable, we may be sure that all of the hearts in the world which are tuned to the same chord will vibrate responsively.

Love is also a creative element which defines our boundaries and limitations. There is an old saying which says every creation carries its own mathematics along with it. You cannot create anything without at the same time creating its relationship to everything else. For instance, when an artist paints a landscape, the contour which he gives to the trees will determine the contours of the sky.

Therefore, whenever you create anything, you will thereby start a chain of causation which will work out in accordance with the thought that started it. And so, we can never be unloved if we are lovable. We set our own chain of causation when we love.

I have always admired the teachings of Marcus Aurelius who said many years ago not to beg your tranquility of another. Don't depend on external supports for your love and happiness.

Independence is the essence of true friendship. We can never fully enjoy a friend until we are wholly independent of his/her affection. We cannot be entirely happy in the thought of keeping anything so long as there exists a fear of losing it.

Love must then become the great magnet of your lives. It will draw to you all that you need. It has an unlimited radius. But before we can control and operate such a powerful force, we must all learn that the greatest secret to all of this is the absolute confidence in the infinite love of God because God is love, the secret to His universal law, which is the love of life. This proposition includes all of the synonyms we use for God, i.e, Love, Truth, Wisdom, Power or any other name.

Let us now turn to the heart. In order to illustrate in perfection, my true feelings about this subject, I must share with you a precious example of the intricacies of love and how it manifested itself to me.

Years ago, a very dear friend of mine became seriously ill. She was afflicted with a health problem which caused the family great concern. I loved her with every fabric of my being. I am sure she loved me as well. She received all of the best medical care which technology had to offer. Her response to treatment was concomitant with the general expectations of the medical attendants.

There was also great family support given to her, especially from her children. And I dare say to you, that if this total support and love which was extended to her was not available, her last days on earth with us would have been very difficult for her. It grieved me to my heart that I could not be more supportive to her as well.

As time passed, it occurred to me that the love and the support which she received from us was coming from our hearts, our own hearts, which is a very real and loving thing to do. But our hearts were on the **outside**.

By living on the outside, we were desiring bodily comfort and good health for her. All of the love and support received by her was only **relief** from difficulty. But difficulty and discomforts return unless we could live in the heart of her heart and sought that which she sought, which may have been a release from us.

This was a thunder-shaking revelation to me and I rebuked it with fervor. But I came to learn that I had to live in her heart and to perhaps discover that health is just the outside expression of perfect life.

At the heart of health is life and life is God, therefore instead of me desiring health and comfort, my desire was to know God's will and to know that the very life that lived in her was God.

I prayed incessantly for her health and comfort, and I must say that the power of prayer is tremendous. But I came to realize I had no right to use the power of God for the purpose of having something done to anything or anyone which I had in mind for them, however beautiful it may seem.

My work for her was simply to know that the Spirit will fulfill its desire in her and for her. I didn't know nor was it possible to know what the Spirit desired of her.

So I learned to live in the heart of the Spirit with her and soon realized that all things would work together for the good of each other. When we learn to live in the heart of things, all things do work together for good.

When I knew that and began to live in the very heart of life, I realized that she could experience both my love and comfort because the Spirit would provide for all of her needs. I knew that she knew she was ready to leave the discomforts of this world. We silently said good-bye to each other as I packed my belongings to move to another city and get my life back on focus. Within a very short period, she died and indeed, a strong liberating force was released, not only for her but for her children and for me.

Her children were free to love and to live in the beautiful spirit she possessed and had shared with them for a lifetime. They were able to make life decisions for their own lives, and within a very short period of time, things worked out very well for all of them.

As Pohaku shared this experience with us, I could see that it was a heavy burden for him to speak about it. There was a pause. I looked around the room and noticed a few people with downcast eyes. Shirley was looking at me with a glistened look of sadness. I knew she had listened with intense purpose to the words of love spoken by Pohaku, and I could feel her thoughts of love directed to me which were received with great glee.

Pohaku closed the discussion by stating that his message (first time he had used this word to describe our discussion) tonight was intended to be introductory and he would gladly invite anyone interested to join in our weekly discussions which were a bit more technical and complex.

He was given a standing ovation led by Aunt Ruth, from the audience. After the applause, the room, which in the beginning, was a chilly cavern crammed with sullen-faced people with dark frowns, became a jumble of ineffable social rapport.

The residents of the hospital were freely interchanging their smiles and handshakes while chatting with the ruddy and important townspeople. The collars of the hospital staff were loosened. There was a complete change of energy in the room.

Pohaku stood aside to himself and observed it all with a look of great satisfaction on his face. He nodded a smile at me as I sat there in energetic optimism. I was excited. Several people had surrounded Aunt Ruth and were both congratulating and thanking her for inviting them. I overheard her say to a sophisticated couple whose wealth was legendary in the area, that they would meet at her house to continue discussing their plans.

As we were leaving the building, the Administrator sauntered up and ejected his hands into Aunt Ruth's while at the same time, in supermarket fashion, saying what a fine meeting it was, and how surprised he was by the residents' behavior, and if she wanted to use the Hall again to just let him know. She gave him her "supermarket" response, "Thanks!"

Eighteen

I Will Build My Church . . .

The following week Aunt Ruth and the sophisticated couple went into town and purchased a small medieval little building. It was a quaint little cottage with thatch roof, half-timbered, and with a conservative ethic. Aunt Ruth said she had been wanting to purchase that building since it was first offered for sale.

Very quickly, she and Uncle Randy refurbished it into a beautiful chapel which could accommodate more than 200 people. Several separate smaller rooms for discussions, offices and comfort facilities, were also constructed.

She went to the hospital to pick up Pohaku and also asked if he would like to invite Mr. Milewski to accompany us. She told him that she had a surprise for him. We drove to the new building and Aunt Ruth invited them to come inside. They silently inspected the accommodations and said how beautiful it was, and Aunt Ruth said very sheepishly, "It's yours."

Pohaku offered a humble, "Thank you," and became transfigured. I saw a strong evidence of holiness in his appearance. Suddenly, he did not appear to be of this world.

He turned to one side and I could visibly see the words, "My Father's house," being spoken as my ears silently said to me, "Now you can go about your father's business."

My body was stricken with a surge of energy which was very much like the energy I had received after the policeman had spoken to me before taking me back to the orphanage. I stood there frozen in time looking at the empty chapel. There sat Deedy on the front row with me next to Shoe and Echols and Booster and Modestine and knappy-headed Cornrows and Eldrine and Jack and Albert and Bobby and Lonnie. Across the aisle sat May and Leyla and Fannie and Mary and Deloris and Ula Mae.

Miss White was there missing the notes on the piano as we all turned to Hymnal No. 31 and sang, *Jesus Keep Me Near The Cross*. There was absolutely no sign of a cross nor Mr. Peay anywhere.

Aunt Ruth remained poised in the majesty which always was her carriage as she shared in his enjoyment.

Mr. Milewski was stunned and speechless except to say, "For a Polish man, this is the first time I have ever been tongue-tied. I'm speechless. I don't know what to say, except thank you and God will bless you for being so kind to us."

Our next meeting was held in the chapel. Uncle Randy assumed the desperate business of the church. The chapel was filled to over-flowing, two hundred people plus more! Aunt Ruth had hired a bus to transport the residents of the hospital after much debate with the Administrator, who finally caved in with his approval, after being faced with a choice of continued employment in that position.

Shirley was among one of the early arrivals and flung herself into assisting in any tasks needed before the meeting started.

I flushed and fluttered when she introduced me to the three people she had brought with her as her "very special friend."
Wow!
I rehearsed each word and listened to their melody as they rang through my ears—*very* and *special* and *friend*.

What did she mean by "special?" I tweaked.

Without any hesitation, Pohaku welcomed the audience, thanked them for coming to our family gathering, thanked Aunt Ruth and started right into the discussion. He began:

I want to say to you that our discussions are not in the least bit an assault on anybody's church or religious beliefs. We wouldn't want to do that, not in the least bit. But we come together to make an assault on your blockages, your resistance. Resistance will be the operating word in our discussion tonight.

We, as exponents of **Autonomic Thought**, now fast becoming to be known as **AT**, are both scientific and spiritual in our relationship with God. We adhere to the laws of nature because they are an inculcation of who we are and what God means to us.

We also adhere to the laws of God because they are the foot-stones of our morality. We see no conflict between the two of them. Conflict comes when we attempt to modify these laws based upon whimsical contingencies and circumstances to fit our own selfish motives. By way of illustration, I will show you how scientifically, both our natural laws and our spiritual laws work hand in hand.

You are familiar with Ohm's formula:

(C) = (E) divided by (R). Let me explain it for those of you who are not familiar. **(C)** means the current of electricity which is to be delivered for any work that is to be done. **(E)** stands for the electric force (electrons) which generates the current, and **(R)** is the resistance or friction offered to the current by the conductor of these electrons, such as the wires through which it flows.

If there is no resistance, the full amount of current generated would be delivered. But without any conductor, no current could be delivered, and therefore there must be **some** resistance, and so the full power of the electric force can never be delivered by the current. The amount that will be delivered is therefore divided by the resistance of the conductor.

And so resistance therefore acts as a restricting force which limits the amount of the original electric force which would be delivered where the work is to be done. But at the same time, no delivery could be affected without it. So resistance has a necessary part to play in the working of the circuit.

Sometimes, even the electric force is so great that it is too much for the resistance which causes a rupturing in the current and must be reduced by breaking the circuit. That's the function of circuit breakers.

Now let us overlay that formula with our spiritual force and let **(C)** = **(E)** divided by **(R)** stand for: **(E)** would be the limitless potential of our eternal spirit; **(C)** would be the channel or current flowing from it, and **(R)** stands for the quality of our thoughts.

We cannot understate the importance of the quality of our thoughts because the whole purpose is to transmute the **unlimited** power of the Spirit into a mode of action. If our thoughts **(R)** are thick with doubt, disbelief, or intractable, then it blocks the channel and renders the flow of the current of the Spirit ineffective.

If they are allowed to degenerate into total disbelief, small mindedness, and denial of the power of the Spirit, we then cancel the originating force altogether. The stream of thought must always have the quality of its source. In other words, if we make **R (which is our thoughts)** greater than **E (which is our source)** in which no currency can flow, we then block out the flow which was sent to us by the Spirit. A thought which is in line with greatness will produce a corresponding result. Thoughts are things and a thought which is disruptive will produce disruptive results, hence all the trouble and confusion in the world.

Our thoughts are perfectly free and we can use them either constructively or destructively, but the immutable laws of nature will not permit us to plant a thought of one kind, and make it bear fruit of another. A fountain that is full of pure water cannot bring forth water which is contaminated unless it becomes modified.

If any of you will recall, the original application to Ohm's Law was spoken many years ago: *According to your faith, be it unto you.*

I'll just give you another simile which may also explain a bit better what I am saying. Let me just say to you that you cannot put in a more powerful stream of water than the size of the pipe through which it flows will allow. Or, to make it even simpler, you can take a horse to water but you can't make him drink.

He closed the meeting rather abruptly and told us to remain and discuss the topic among ourselves. Tossing the keys to the Cadillac to me, Aunt Ruth asked me if I would take him back to the hospital. She wanted to remain and do some organizing among the attendants.

As I turned to leave the chapel, she yelled to Shirley, "Why don't you go with him. Go on, and I'll get a ride home from here when we finish."

We took Pohaku back home in complete silence. When we reached his building, I asked if anything was wrong.

"Not a thing. I just wanted to let things begin to take place on their own. I feel very confident that your Aunt Ruth will have things organized and things here will be well on their way. We can now say that the horses have been lead to the water and I must begin to prepare myself to take care of some other things now."

I suddenly realized that sometimes Pohaku would go someplace by himself in order to be alone. He would reappear with an unbelievable show of strength and enthusiasm. One day I asked him where did he go when he disappeared from us.

He answered, "Into my closet to pray and to give thanks to my Father for the many blessings He has given to me, and most of all I thank Him for choosing me to act as an emissary to conduct His business."

As he said these words, my mind zoomed forward with frightened clarity. These were the words of Jesus that somehow I had studied and I remembered how I felt when these words were spoken. I began to get the same feeling with him as I did with Andrew—that he was a heavenly figure and would soon be leaving us. My heart saddened. Yet I also felt a jolt of enlightenment because I really felt that even if he did leave me, he, like Andrew was not really gone from me. I straightened my back and starched my eyes in a glare at him as he walked inside the building and silently shouted to myself, **"No, it couldn't be. He can't be..."**

Shirley looked at me in great astonishment as I automatically began to walk across the lawn with my feet not touching the ground. I was brought back into this world when I felt the touch of a human hand upon mine. I looked around and there sat Shirley next to me. I asked her how long she had been there. She said at least five minutes.

"I followed you to where you were going thinking that something was wrong with you. You came right to this bench and sat down and didn't say a word. You looked like you were staring into outer space. I figured you didn't want to talk so I just sat here beside you."

I looked towards the lake. I looked at the bench and I realized that this was the same bench I sat and talked with Andrew when we first met and where this all began.

I turned to Shirley and without any words spoken, I kissed her with such handsome ruthlessness, that even Hollywood would have wanted to re-cast our performance. I am positive that the feeling which began to generate between us was not just a "booty" feeling.

From then on, we began to date. Aunt Ruth "adopted" her as her niece. Her stepmother refused to have anything to do with her, stating that I had influenced her mind and brainwashed her into sinning and we were both going to burn up in hell on Judgement Day when the Lord comes and take His people home.

She seemed to find it quite amusing to watch her stepmother conducting the business of her life. I always stressed to her that she should not put her down nor criticize her belief and to never argue with her about it.

The meetings were now beginning to become too large for the small chapel to handle so Aunt Ruth decided that it would better if they were held on Sundays instead of Wednesday.

On the first Sunday, the chapel could not accommodate all of the audience so the meeting rooms and the offices were pressed into service. Pohaku's reputation began to spread like wildfire. He was in constant demand to speak in college religion classes and to other groups and churches throughout Massachusetts, Connecticut, and New York City. The attendance at the chapel continued to grow, so Aunt Ruth decided to have two sessions on Sunday.

Within six months, a third session was held at seven thirty in the morning to accommodate the early risers. Pohaku was tireless and enthusiastic in all of the sessions. It appeared that he had some source of energy which never expired or even wavered. Mr. Milewski started a Wednesday evening study group at the hospital and it soon became very successful.

A student study group was started at Radcliff by Brenda, one of the girls who used to speak to Aunt Ruth when we first went to the hospital to visit. She had now reenrolled at Radcliff and was doing very well. With all of these new groups and sessions being conducted everywhere, it seemed as if **AT** was what people had long been hungering and thirsting for.

Aunt Ruth was seen by many as its parent and Pohaku its heartbeat. She was very adept in managing its rapid growth and quick to reply to all inquiries that it was not a religion of authority nor was it a one-person religion.

She explained to people that **AT** was a religion based upon the natural tendencies of nature in harmony with all of its laws. It affirmed that the will of its Creator is good, and that life is beautiful and bountiful. It allowed people to sit in judgement and sift and weigh and decide for themselves and it made an appeal to their intellect.

The followers of **AT** were all students of the truth. It was not a cult, nor was it mystery or miracle. It was a scaffolding but not an intellectual crutch. Pohaku had repeatedly stated that the individual who mistook the scaffolding for the real building was a specialist in scaffolding.

The distinguishing feature of **AT** was its use of truth and rationality while at the same time making the realization that truth could never be caught and crystallized into a formula.

AT would never be labelled or reduced into an "ism" or an "ite" because as Pohaku had taught us, eventually the label would be stripped away along with the scaffolding, and then the timber and plywood of the ritual (ism) and rite (ite) would have to go. With **AT**, the truth was lived instead of arguing it.

I had learned quite a lot during this time of growth and development and felt very good and satisfied that I had just a little to do with its birth. I didn't spend any time with the Broomfields except with Linda. They seemed to have disappeared with a puff right from my mind and from my life.

As I sat reading in my room one day, Linda burst through the door more resplendent than ever. With a big grin on her teeth, she shoved an envelop in my hand and said, "This is something you would be interested in, go ahead and open it."

I ripped it open and unfolded its contents which was an official looking document embroidered with the fancy edges and embossed with a government seal. It's headlines glared:

State of North Carolina Certificate of Live Birth.
I read it rapidly and there it was:
Name of live birth child: AMOS BROOMFIELD.
Name of father: AMOS BROOMFIELD AKA WILLIAM.
"Oh, Wow! "
I read it again, this time very slowly. I read it again, even more slowly. I turned it over to see if there were some more. Each time I read it, it said the same thing: AMOS BROOMFIELD, Amos Broomfield, Amos Broomfield, Amos...Broomfield...

Neither the Hammer of Thor nor the Bolt of Ajax could have shaken me more. I gave it another look, then grabbed Linda so tight, a gush of air flooded out her mouth while at the same time jumping up and down yelling, "Amos, Amos, Amos," as loud as I could.

She also started to yell with me, "Amos, Amos, get off my foot."

"Oh!"

This was the crowning event of my life. For me, this was the day I was born. I was real, a real live person. I was alive. I actually existed. I had parents. A mother and a father. My mother's name was Helen and my father's name was Amos, same as mine. Here it was! The State told me so. According to the date of birth, I was sixteen.

I now felt the same happiness as when Shoe's parents or Eldrine's or Joe Lewis' parents came out to visit them. I could now come out from beneath the front porch and hold my own parents' hands and eat the candy and wear the new shoes and socks and overalls and sweaters. I also knew that Shoe and the rest of them were at this very moment sharing this happiness with me. I really missed them. I wished they were with me to see the joy painted on my face.

I graduated from high school with excellent grades and had no idea what I would do upon graduation. Shirley was going down to New York to attend the elite all-girls Sarah Lawrence College with all expenses paid by Aunt Ruth and Uncle Randy. Ronald was studying the exam to go to med school. I just didn't know what I would do.

On Monday morning, as we were having breakfast, the doorbell rang. It was a messenger from Western Union with a telegram from Manhattan addressed to Aunt Ruth. She hurriedly opened and read it and it seemed as if all life fled from her, both arms fell lifeless to her side as the telegram fell to the floor. Uncle Randy picked it up and groaned, "Oh, no!"

It was a message to inform us that Pohaku had died. He died of cardiac arrest on stage while in the process of giving a speech to the student body at New York City College. The officials at NYCC were asking if a representative could come and attend to his affairs.

Aunt Ruth and I flew down and were met at the hospital by his son and other men dressed in grey flannel suits and short-brimmed hats. He told us that he would handle things and there was no need for us to stick around.

"What about funeral and burial arrangements," Aunt Ruth asked.

"They have all been taken care of."

"Can we see him? I'd very much like to see him for just a little while."

"The body has already gone. I'm just here to take care of some paperwork. I guess the only thing you can do is to go back to Massachusetts. Incidentally, how are things going with the church? I understand it is becoming popular."

"Things are coming along real fine," she said heading towards the door.

We flew back to Boston. During the flight, I thought to myself, Pohaku, gone, just like that. Not a trace of any personal belongings, not even his body could be found. He just left us. I looked out of the windows into the billowing clouds as the plane dipped and climbed through the turbulent skies. I was halfway expecting to see him and Andrew there.

Since no words were spoken about him at the time of his death, or no services or ceremonies conducted, my mind began to think of him in eulogy. I strongly felt that he was a messenger of God whom I had the privilege to meet. He had the same simple lucidity and gentle humanity, the same effort to discard complicated non-essentials as Jesus. Only in the intimacy of his own "home" at the mental institution did he wholly reveal his innate modesty and simplicity of character. I felt very privileged to be included in his "humble world."

Here alone, glamored with his radiating friendship, was shown the wealth of his richly-stored mind equipped by nature to deal logically with the most profound and abstruse questions of life. Here in this "nut house" was his proof of greatness, his unassuming superiority, his humanity, his keen sense of honor, his wit and humor, his generosity and all the characteristics of a rare gentleman, a kindly philosopher, teacher, and a true friend.

I continued to think about his lectures which were given with the ease and gracefulness of a logician to strip a subject bare of all non-essentials and excessive verbiage, and to exhibit the gleaming jewels of truth and reality in splendid simplicity. These supreme qualities gave to him a personality of charming naivete that challenged attention and compelled confidence and affection towards him. His sincerity was beyond question. However much a person might have differed from him in opinions and discussions, at least one never doubted his profound faith and complete devotion to truth.

Tenderness, tolerance, and the opinions of others, dwelt in his every word and deed. Yet his consideration of others did not paralyze the strength of his power to strike hard blows at wrong and error. I am certain that these were the reasons Aunt Ruth was immediately fascinated with him.

I asked Aunt Ruth why was he called Pohaku. It seemed to be a funny name, like the name of some foreigner. She said Pohaku is the Hawaiian pronunciation for Peter.

"Peter! Peter!" I exclaimed. "Wasn't he the disciple whom Jesus said, 'Upon this rock I will build my church?'

"Yes he was," said Aunt Ruth.

She gave me a surprised look as she asked me if I wanted to take a trip with her.

"Yes, where to?"

"I'm thinking about going to visit my sisters in Hawaii."

"Hawaii! You have some relatives in Hawaii too?"

"Yes, I have two sisters living there. I think you would like living there."

"Me? In Hawaii? That's called Paradise; the Paradise of the Pacific with all of the hula girls, coconuts and beaches. I could stay there?"

"We'll see."

Nineteen

Paradise . . .

Three weeks later and after twelve hours of flying, we heard the voice of the pilot over the intercom, "Aloha ladies and gentlemen, we are now on our descent into the beautiful State of Hawaii. Welcome to Paradise." I wanted to jump out and start running. I couldn't wait until we landed.

As we walked through the Honolulu airport, the sweet fragrance of flowers was intoxicating. Music was being played by an incredibly beautiful Hawaiian lady accompanied by a handsome dark-skinned Hawaiian man playing a ukulele. A couple of Hawaiian girls who were not dressed in long formless missionary garb but stapled with grass skirts were seductively snaking their bronze hips in a hula dance. They were singing to me:

Come my love,
With me,
Across the sea,
Return to Paradise.

Come with me,
And find,
Your peace of mind,

Return to Paradise.
Velvet moon above,
Evil turns to love,
Love evermore.

Those words were cemented in my mind as we were greeted by two ladies with arm-loads of flower leis. One of the ladies, the oldest, looked exactly like Aunt Ruth.

"This is my sister, Johnnie, and this is my sister **Marva**, your Aunt Johnnie and Aunt Marva," said Aunt Ruth after they had stopped hugging and kissing each other.

We left the airport and drove along the most beautiful coastline in the whole wide world. I said to myself, "Do people actually live here? This is the Garden of Eden, even better than Eden because I'm here."

Aunt Johnnie was married to a Filipino man who loved her very much. I could close my eyes and see a complete replication of she and Uncle Padello as with Uncle Randy and Aunt Ruth. Aunt Marva was a bit reserved and didn't talk much in the presence of Aunt Johnnie but would talk your ears off when you are alone with her. Aunt Johnnie lived in a sprawling newly constructed house in the Valley of Kalihi with an uninterrupted view of the mountains, the ocean, and the beaches. I simply can't say how beautiful it was. I was given my own room and my own **bathroom!** So this was the Kingdom of Heaven! And to think, I would be living here.

Aunt Ruth had to return to Massachusetts after three weeks of going to hula shows, night clubs, luas, boat rides, shopping malls, fancy restaurants, visiting historic volcanoes, lolling on the beaches, and chatting endlessly with Aunt Johnnie and Aunt Marva.

I hated to see her go. She was the only real mother I had. She opened up my life for me. She saw the value of the human spirit in me and tapped into my reservoir of love which we shared openly and honestly. But most of all, she epitomized a clear and concise manifestation of truth. She was my treasure.

Aunt Johnnie did not miss a heartbeat from where Aunt Ruth left off. She was "Aunt Ruth" living in paradise which doubled the pleasure for me. She and Uncle Padello had no children. I became her son and she, my mother. My only concern was could I be "son-enough" for her.

Just like Aunt Ruth, we'd spend hours sitting at the kitchen table chatting. There was never a doubt in her mind as to what I would do with my life. She had my life all planned which began firstly by going to college. Education to her was first and foremost.

Both she and Aunt Marva were the linchpins of the small black community in Hawaii. Aunt Marva had started the NAACP Chapter there, and was very involved in the politics of the State. Aunt Johnnie was the support person for any cause she firmly believed in.

All of "high society" as well as the "extremely low society" beat pathways to her door. She donated money to a young man who was running a junk-yard and wanted to run for mayor of Honolulu. She believed in him and practically single-handedly supported his campaign. He was successful and served as mayor for more than twenty years.

She had sponsored three black female students from the slums of Chicago who were gifted athletes and wanted to attend college and become track stars. She paid all of their expenses for four years at the University of Hawaii. One of the girls was on the United States track team with Wilma Rudolph in the Melbourne Olympics.

Aunt Johnnie never held her tongue when she talked to me. She told me emphatically that I had a choice if I wanted to stay with her, and it was simply this: "You can go and hang out in the bars down on Hotel Street and run with the pimps and prostitutes and do anything you wish out there; but if you do, I don't ever want to see you again. If you choose to do that, I want you to be the best pimp out there, but don't come to me for help. Or, you can stay here, and if you want to go to college, I will guarantee that you do so. But you must make a choice. You can't do both."

"Yes ma'am."

I enrolled at the University of Hawaii and graduated with two double majors, politics-sociology and religion-philosophy. I was a starting running back on the football team for three years, and a student senator on the student government.

When I had some time to myself, I would steal away to my own little private "home" I had discovered. It was on a deserted beach on the outskirts of Waikiki beneath a Coast Guard lighthouse. There were some small caverns among the cliffs overlooking the beach below and the vast expanse of the blue Pacific Ocean.

It was the most tranquil and peaceful place on earth for me. I would climb up the cliffs and sit on the overhanging ledge and stay there all weekend. Nobody but Aunt Johnnie knew where I was.

As I sat there one Saturday morning watching the fishing boats leaving the harbor to go out for their daily catch, I looked through the clouds to a spot just beyond the horizon—beyond where the earth meets the sky, and I saw in very plain view, two men dressed in Biblical garb with long and flowing beards walking and conversing with themselves.

They never looked in my direction. One of the men was wearing a floor length white robe, the other was dressed in blue. I became mesmerized with the familiarity with these two men. They looked like some people whom I had seen and met before. They seemed to have the same familiarity with me. There was no distance between us. Rather, there was a closeness that was real and true and comforting. Thoughts of Andrew and Pohaku swam through my mind as I visited with them. I knew that it was them who had come to visit me. I was comforted with the thought that I had a real spiritual connection with the truth and wisdom which was granted to me.

I finished the University of Hawaii and made applications to about a dozen schools including UCLA, Stanford, McGill, Cal Berkeley, Princeton, and Chicago. Harvard was not included. I received notices of acceptances from all of them.

I visited UCLA and wasn't satisfied. Berkeley didn't appeal to me and neither did Stanford. I went to Princeton and discovered that the professor I wanted to study with had left and gone to Harvard. I decided to stop by Harvard on my way to Worcester to visit Aunt Ruth and Uncle Randy and see if I could find Professor Adam Curle, an Englishman who was exiled from South Africa because of his support for the African National Congress (ANC).

He was the world's leading scholar in peace studies. He had known both Nehru and Ghandi and was trying to get schools to start teaching the techniques of peace and nonviolence. I was lucky. He was located in the Graduate School of Education. It was during the latter part of July when I met him and told him that I wanted to study with him but it was too late for the upcoming fall term.

"Poppycock," he exclaimed. "Do you want to come to Harvard?"

"Yes!"

"Then you can come. I just received word from the Dean that one student will be going to work in the White House and she won't be coming so that leaves a slot for you. We only take in twelve new students each year. I'll tell the Dean that the class is full."

I pinched myself to see if this was all true as I skidded across the state to Worcester to tell Aunt Ruth. She was absolutely ecstatic. The tears in her eyes were filled with bucket loads of glee. We both got on the telephone and shouted the news to Aunt Johnnie. We really didn't need the telephone as loud as we both were yelling.

I asked Aunt Ruth if I could make a trip down south to visit the orphanage. She immediately called the airlines for my ticket. I asked if she wouldn't mind if I took the bus. She said, "Okay, I understand."

I dressed in clothing which were befitting for the trip. I only had on my possession my bus ticket, one dollar and twenty five cents, and some chicken sandwiches she had made for me. I sat in approximately the same seat location as I did coming to Massachusetts. As the bus started southward, I gazed out the windows at the telephone poles and the trees as they whizzed by. I counted the rocks, read the billboards and car license plates, gawked at the buildings, held my breath through the tunnels and held my pee as we crossed over the bridges.

The bus arrived in North Carolina at three o'clock in the

morning. As I sat in the bus station waiting for the dawn before seeking a ride to the orphanage, I looked for the colored section. It was gone. The South had been integrated. I hadn't noticed it while riding the bus. I hadn't even noticed I wasn't told to get up and move to another seat towards the back. When we arrived in Washington, D.C., things seemed as normal as if this had been their way of life years before.

As the sun peeked through the trees, I noticed an old man sitting across from me reading a newspaper. He also had a few books tucked in his coat pockets. I asked him if he could tell me how to get to the orphanage.

He looked at me with a puzzled look in his eye. He asked, "What orphanage you talking about? You talking about that industrial school where that man used to beat them children?"

"Yes sir."

"Son they done closed that place up and ran that old nigger out of town. They said he beat up one of them kids so bad that the kid died. He knocked-up two of the girls out there. Two of my grandchildren used to be out there."

"Oh, no." I wondered which kids they were.

"Yeah they closed that place up maybe three years ago and made it into a crazy house. They put all of the crazy people out there now."

I looked at him and couldn't hold back the tears. He said to me in a very soft and comforting voice; "You were one of them kids weren't you?"

"Yes, sir."

"I'll tell you what, I ain't got nothing to do today. Why don't we just take a ride out there and let you see the place."

We got into his very old pickup truck and drove there. My heart was pounding as we approached the dirt road off the main highway which lead to the campus. The first building which shot out at me like it was standing guard was the main administration building where Mr. and Mrs. Peay stayed. Then there was the Big Boys Dormitory, the Big Girls Dorm and the Baby Cottage.

I sat in the truck glued to the seat. The Baby Cottage greeted me with maternalistic familiarity. It sat there hunched as a mother hen smothering her little ones.

Miss Pounds still vibrated throughout the place. Deedy's pee still scented the air. Booster's cache was stuffed someplace inside. Henry and Juanita were still getting it on in the dirty linen closet. Leyla's little dirty drawers still had me throbbing. Ula Mae was still chasing Snipper around the playroom. Shoe and Echols were still beating up each other. Joe Lewis' grunts could still be heard, and the front porch said good-bye to May and myself.

I looked across the lawn at the new residents which had been stamped "crazy" and I saw people who were talking to each other, some were playing and weeping and hugging and kissing and reading and listening and loving one another and all of the many other things that humans do.

The old man seemed to display some spiritual connection with them as he gave me a perplexing look when I asked him if we could leave.

"You sure you want to leave? You only been here for twenty minutes."

"Yes sir. Please lets go."

He drove slowly through the campus and as we were leaving, the residents were all smiling and waving to us as we drove by. He took me back to the bus station. I thanked him and extended my right hand to shake his hand. He extended his left hand saying that the right arm was paralyzed.

As I slid out of the truck, he looked me in the eyes and said, "Son, I just want to say a few words to you. No matter how hard life has been to you, don't let it throw you and get you down. You just have to keep on plugging and praying. You got to hang in there and keep God in all of the things that you do. Do what you can to help other people and lightened their loads and bring a little joy into their lives. You seems like a bright young man and I'm counting on you to do the best you can as you go about doing your father's business."

What's your name son?

"Amos, Amos Broomfield."

When he heard my name it appeared as if he had been struck by a bolt of lightening. The stale look of the ancients in his eyes were replaced with a youthful beam which seemed to be affixed about one inch above my head. I asked him, "What's your name, sir?"

"Hrummn. Ah, William. They just call me Willie!"

I started to ask him what was his last name, but somehow my voice box was empty. No words could be marshalled. My mouth was just an open cave full of cobwebs and dusted with aridity.

He drove off. Zoom!

Naw... it couldn't be. He couldn't be...

As the bus headed north, I thought to myself that knowing the truth was not an easy matter. It could sometimes be rather rough and downright nasty at times, but its foundations were never shaken in me. I knew that Andrew and Pohaku were pretty rough on God at times, but they only bolstered in me the true underpinnings of my faith in God. They also rattled me out of the rat trap reasoning of what had been taught to me as religion. They taught me that this was not merely a walk in faith, rather, it was a faithful walk which included developing and utilizing all of the talents and gifts given to me by my Creator which harmonize with all of the other immense intelligences of nature.

I was saddened with the thought that Andrew's brilliance was not shared with other members of the family. Most troubling to me was that my mother and sister Roseanne, enrobed in the cloak of their limited views and missionary zeal, chose to fight shadows rather than seek the unlimited wardrobe of truth. I had hoped that they would someday come to the realization that truth needs no torch-bearers; that it is bountiful and has an unlimited wardrobe and we should not insist that it is always dressed in the colors of our choice.

My overriding sadness was that they were unable to share Andrew's view that truth has many names, and the best known name for it is something which I had always wanted to give and receive in both the orphanage and with this family, and that name is "Love."

Once again, Andrew's words began to vibrate in my memory when he had spoken to me about the family and not to be deceived by appearances. I remembered him telling me that spiritual work required spiritual tools and when the soil was ready, flowers grew. He had told me that some of the finest flowers bloomed in the desert as well as in the hothouses and that God was the gardener and my only responsibility was to cultivate my own field.

He also knew how disappointed I was with my family and he told me that my highest accomplishments will often come through my deepest disappointments. Disappointments, he said, were just the discovery of obstacles to ways I should not travel. With these words in mind, I thought about how my family is very much like the life-cycle of a tree. I followed the course of its growth from the seed to fruition, through its root life, the trunk, the branch, the leaf, bud, blossom, and fruit.

Looking at the components of my family, my father with a missing hand was not unlike the tree's broken trunk. My mother's sap pulsed in all of its branches. Andrew, and the others were the branches, buds, blossoms, and fruits. And, while thinking of the components of the tree and members of my family, I then asked myself at what point can I claim that one component is any higher than the other. They are all equally important for the full development of both. The Creator is just as present in the mud of the root as He is in the sunlight of the branches.

I then concluded that there is no individual, community, nation, period of time, or work of art that is wholly without fault. Therefore, why should I be so quick to condemn or commend just because my taste for certain things is gratified or offended? Andrew and Pohaku had taught me through the lessons of AT that praise and blame are both undesirable to a person who knows that no true judgement can ever be reached except when we judge ourselves.

I remembered his admonition to me not to feel sorry for myself or for others. Rather, I should learn that at every moment of human existence, each individual was experiencing exactly that which his stage of development required, and just as soon as that lesson was learned, that experience passed and gave you the freedom to move on to other experiences.

On the bus I mused:

I'm leaving this place again with a newly found freedom based upon a myriad of precious experiences. Again, headed for Massachusetts, only this time I've got my identity intact. I know who my **real** parents are. I know the pains and anguish which accompany the searching and the seeking and the finding. This time I'm headed for Harvard—*that citadel of truth and knowledge*, land of the icons bearing the "Ve Ri Tas" stamp, and yet I'm humbled by the confidence that I will do well, for I know that I'm not alone as the Spirit of my Creator goes with me.

The Author

A previously published author, English Bradshaw is a writer, educator, and independent consultant. He holds a Master of Education and a Master of Public Administration degree from Harvard University. From the University of Hawaii, he holds both a Master and a Bachelor of Arts degree and is presently completing his Ph.D. requirements in Political Science.

Look for English Bradshaw's forthcoming book, *Lifting The Veil*, scheduled for release in August 1996 by Duncan & Duncan, Inc.